PRAISE FOR
WALKING THE
LEADERSHIP TIGHTROPE

Chris Ice has created a marvelous read that represents proof positive that effective leadership can lead to organizational success. He provides all of us with a roadmap for success that involves clinging to faith, family, and career during times of chaos and crisis. He eloquently describes a personal journey that will inspire leaders of today and tomorrow to keep moving forward, regardless of the obstacles that confront them. This work should be considered a "must-read" for leadership classes and conferences in any academic or organizational setting.

— Dr. Thomas Kelly, Chair of Business Department, Franciscan University of Steubenville

Chris Ice's book is compelling. He takes us on a journey of triumph and tragedy with a mix of common sense, leadership, and faith. Veteran and aspiring leaders alike will benefit from his wisdom and encouragement. I moved through this book with attention, interest, and speed.

— Dr. Richard Ludwick, President, University of St. Thomas-Houston

This is not a book about high-brow leadership concepts, it is real and personal. It is not about the American Dream; it is about God's dream for each of our lives. There is certainly trial and error as part of each of our journeys in life, but Chris Ice gives it to us from the "inside-out", not the "outside- in." Life experience matters and just like when Peter stepped out of the boat to walk on water at the beckoning of Jesus, we too must step out and take risks that may not make much sense. Ambition is important as well as virtue, but we cannot do anything without stepping out into the "unknown" and allowing our gifts to flourish, take root, and thus learn from our mistakes. All is gift and this book, personal as it is, will inspire all to realize that each of us will be challenged to lead in some manner whether at work or with family and yes, that is a tightrope for sure.

— Lamar Hunt, President & Owner, Kansas City Mavericks & Owner, Kansas City Chiefs

This book is Chris to the tee. Calm, thought-provoking, joy-filled even during tragedies, goal oriented, brave, and grounded in his faith and family.

I am fortunate to have had the opportunity to experience portions of his book in our personal interactions as my leader. I remember when I met him for my interview. I had a book in my briefcase, Call to Joy, that I shared with him because of his kindness and ability to connect right from the beginning due to his

WALKING

THE

LEADERSHIP TIGHTROPE

HOW TO BALANCE CAREER AND FAMILY THROUGH THE CHAOS OF CRISIS

CHRISTOPHER P. ICE

BRIGHTRAY
PUBLISHING®

We help busy professionals write and publish their stories
to distinguish themselves and their brands.

(407) 287-5700 | Winter Park, FL
info@BrightRay.com | www.BrightRay.com

ISBN: 978-1-956464-35-1

Published in the United States of America.
BrightRay Publishing ® 2023

gentleness. Because he was such a good listener and had a welcoming heart, I probably shared more than I should have during an interview (allows others to be transparent). We ended up talking about positivity, energy levels, and St. Joseph.

What I respect the most about Chris was his ability to remain focused on the agreed upon priorities. Yes, I needed to increase enrollment, but he wanted to do it the right way with the right students. When we had our weekly meetings, he always asked how he could help and allowed me to make the decisions based on trust of my prior business experience. Chris knew how to run a business and lead people to achieve more than they even knew they could.

The book was emotional for me. My heart was breaking during times of struggles and then full of joy with laughter for the wins through perseverance. Chris does not give up. Seeing him at daily morning Mass or in the adoration chapel saying his rosary was always a delight. He is a big man and commands respect with his presence. To see the humble, quiet, gentle side made him even a stronger leader.

I call Chris when I need advice. He helped coach me through a recent job promotion (to a triple financial advantage). He has coached me through a consecration, the hiring of my first Director, conflict with another Cabinet member, and my next promotion. Chris is a coach. He knows business. He knows life. He knows balance. He knows Christ.

— **Dr. Dee Gipson, Vice-President of Enrollment,**
Catholic University of America

Chris Ice has effectively utilized lessons learned from his remarkable life story to provide aspiring leaders with a blueprint for success, not only for companies or organizations, but for life itself.

— Jeff Webb, Varsity Brands founder and former Chairman and CEO, Publisher of *Human Events* and *The Post Millennial*

There are those who succumb to negativity and adversity—who endlessly complain about life's curveballs. But there are also true leaders, who hit curveballs right out of the park. Christopher Ice is one of those leaders. His faith-based principles of leadership are sure to benefit anyone in a position of authority, whether that is a father of a family or the president of a university. Walking the Leadership Tightrope is a training manual for meaningful success.

— John Clark, Catholic apologist and father of nine

I would like to dedicate this book in memory of two people. First, my maternal grandmother, Frances M. Cawley, whose life has always been a great inspiration throughout my career and a great example of leadership in my life. Second, my late wife Mary K. Ice, the mother of my seven children who supported me for 32 years in marriage and throughout my business career.

TABLE OF CONTENTS

INTRODUCTION

My grandmother's house always smelled like a bakery. She was constantly working in her kitchen, baking wedding cakes for a living. Some of my fondest childhood memories were in her house, where we would eat leftover cake scraps straight from the pans or spread different types of icing she had in her fridge on little white soda crackers. None of her eight kids or thirty-plus grandkids went without a cake for their birthday. She even baked my wedding cake; she was 80 when she hauled it all the way from Kansas City to Nebraska in 109-degree weather in the back of my brother's 1981 Toyota Celica.

She lived one mile away ("as the crow flies") from my childhood home in Lawrence, KS, and would stop by every morning at 7:30 AM to pick me up to serve Mass for our Irish parish priest. She never missed a day and on those 12-minute drives to St. John the Evangelist Catholic Church, even though I was only seven and usually half-asleep in the front passenger seat, I appreciated her incredible wisdom, her insight on life, and her deep faith. These lessons have stuck with me throughout my life and career—theological virtues of faith, hope, and charity, and character virtues of perseverance, magnanimity, humility, prudence, honesty, and courage—and that's just the beginning.

My maternal grandmother.

I was constantly inspired by this little elderly woman, this cake-baking entrepreneur, this devout Catholic who prayed the rosary daily, who in her younger years had a formal education that ended in the 8th grade when she was sent out as a housekeeper and nanny to earn money for the family. She was a leader and a provider who did what she had to do to raise eight kids through the Great Depression while my grandfather worked in the fields on the small family farm. She wasn't a big talker (she was German, so you know how it goes), but she was an amazing mother and grandmother, an extraordinarily hard worker, and one of the holiest women I have ever known.

She and my wonderful parents were the foundation for my future success as a collegiate baseball player and then a baseball coach, a commercial insurance executive, an owner of a healthcare company, a CEO of a non-profit, the

President and CEO of a Catholic university in Florida, and now, the founder and CEO of an executive coaching and consulting company.

There's always been something about leadership positions that have reeled me in. My faith has led me to these in ways that surprise me—but each opportunity has shaped my thinking and has helped me grow as a person and as a leader.

I have learned over time, leaders are not born; *they are made*. Great leaders have a unique internal drive, a great sense of urgency, and a positive outlook on life. They fight through intense adversity, are honest, and act with integrity. Influential leaders are introverts *and* extroverts and have a high level of self-confidence. They believe they can do just about anything and are not afraid to fail.

Leaders are sculpted with these traits through experience. But the motivation comes from within. People don't always understand them and question their motives. Great leaders are accused of being "dreamers" and "out of touch with reality," but the right word to describe them is "visionaries." Many people who want comfort and assurance in the midst of chaos fail to see how leaders can effectively navigate each situation they encounter.

I've been in many meetings with small-minded thinkers who can't put their own egos aside to move the organization forward. That's because they live in a silo; they're self-serving. A leader has to be strong and ensure ideas fit with their vision and the mission of the organization and resist the temptation to allow distractions of those not buying in. No organization can be cohesive or grow without a culture that nurtures big ideas, one where everyone is on board with the mission instead of creating chaos behind the scenes with gossip, unhealthy conversations, and selfish agendas. Great leaders find ways to weed these people out, but it is not always easy to see these harmful elements of your organization.

Something within me was always looking for ways to lead. In the first year of my insurance career, I recall a friend asking me what my career goal was. Without hesitation, I answered: "To be the president." I wanted to get there with the highest degree of integrity and only if my company wanted me in that position. My friend stepped back, smirked, and said I was really ambitious. But it's not about dreaming too big—I knew that if I didn't have this goal in front of me at all times, I might lose my desire to keep succeeding. That was my internal drive. There was something in my gut that told me I would be a president one day, and I let that positivity train guide me. Every day at work, I asked the executives in my company a lot of questions, listened to others around me, and learned from mentors who had achieved high levels of success. I did my best to avoid negative people who complained incessantly—they were nothing more than barriers to my goals.

In the end, I never dreamed that my goal of being a president would be attained at a Catholic university in Florida. I'd also never dreamed that everything I had learned about leadership would be severely tested in the middle of an unprecedented global pandemic—and during a major personal tragedy too. I was able to lead my organization through one of their and my toughest times in history through strong faith, a laser-focus on the goals established, a high level of integrity, and a strong will to lead the organization through the challenges, just as I had done my whole career.

Through all this, I realized something important: *a leader creates a vision for the mission.* If you want people to buy into your mission, to say, "I want to be involved in this," "I want to work for this," or "I would love to donate to this organization," a leader needs to create a vision for it that really sets it apart. They need to define that purpose and start capturing stories that justify why others want to be involved. You learn this by asking questions and listening.

But to make this a reality, to oil these wheels of vision and mission, you need grease—and that's a positive outlook. Initially, you find the good things and reinforce them even in the midst of negativity. Once your positive energy gets the mission moving forward, people follow. That's when you truly become a leader who inspires.

Just like a tightrope walker, you must have the mental toughness to endure, but it is only through years of experience that you can prepare for a major crisis. You have to focus on the task at hand, and cultivate optimism at all levels as the crisis ensues. There are always seemingly unsolvable problems that stand in the way, but instead of giving in to despair and wondering how anyone can possibly solve them, I focus all my attention on getting through them. I give all my attention to the problem at hand and to my goal that stands in the distance. That's where my energy goes.

As a leader, if you can make everybody else focus on that vision with you, then success will follow. You have to implement the discipline to keep yourself grounded and calm with the mental toughness to not waver in a crisis. When everyone starts believing in the mission, you *will* find a way. You will create an emotional charge and momentum that can solve any issue that is thrown at you. That's the power of a vision, a mission, and a positive outlook. When I lead, I'm ultimately saying, "I'm going to work hard toward this vision with a positive mindset, and if it's God's will, it will happen."

When I was in the midst of grieving my wife's passing while leading the university through COVID-19 shutdowns, my positive outlook and strong faith helped me grow and gave me the strength to lead. One Bible verse especially guided me through many tribulations that have come my way—Romans 5:3-4, "Not only so, but we also glory in our sufferings, because we know that suffering produces perseverance; perseverance, character; and character, hope." Remembering that through each trial, I can (and must) persevere, gave me the hope I needed to move forward.

When my wife passed on the afternoon of April 30th, 2020, I had to shelve my own grief for a while. It wasn't healthy, but I didn't have a choice—the pandemic was upon us and big decisions had to be made at the university or people would lose their jobs; my kids were mourning and had no one but me to lean on in our new town, and everything around me never stopped moving. I was responsible for my family, four (of seven) children who were still living at home, more than 300 faculty and staff members, some 1,200 students, and, in many respects, the entire community beyond the university, which was an estimated 8,000 people. I was a leader in my family and at work. And I couldn't let anyone down.

Every day, I walked the tightrope—I had my grieving family on one side and my university and work on the other. People needed answers *now*, and while they certainly were sympathetic, no one could truly understand my predicament. The one thing that kept me walking straight and steady was my faith. I've walked the leadership tightrope for ages now but never more so than during 2020 when my personal life and work life were completely upended. But through perseverance, a vision and a mission, a positive mindset, hope, and faith, I was able to walk the tightrope and make it to the present successfully.

I did my best to help my children move forward but struggled mightily. The university secured the highest fundraising year ever at $22.5 million along with the highest enrollment in history in the fall semester of 2021. I kept Ave Maria open during the global pandemic with very low cases on campus, and housed happy and safe students, along with faculty and staff who were glad to have some semblance of normality. Later, after stepping down as president, I started my own company: Ice Executive Coaching and Consulting. All in the midst of tragedies, crises, and chaos, while walking the leadership tightrope.

This is the story of how I did it, with experience, perseverance, and God's guidance. And here's how you too can walk that leadership tightrope to success.

CHAPTER ONE

A Kansas Upbringing

Picture this: you're seven years old. It's a snowy Saturday morning. You're nestled under the warm covers, happy and excited for the day: no school, no classes, no homework, and a chance to play in the snow later. You pull your blankets up to your chin and curl up into a content, sleepy ball. But then, you hear the dreaded distant sound of a quick knock on the door, your mother comes in and she's on a mission: Grandma's here and ready to take you to serve Mass.

As a young boy, Mass wasn't necessarily how I wanted to spend my Saturdays or weekdays during the summers. But my grandmother was an exceptionally faith-driven woman, and she took me every day to help our local Irish pastor at my church. My uncle was a missionary priest, and I was well aware of the expectation to follow in my uncle's footsteps, carry on the tradition, and become the next priest in my family.

While I didn't enjoy waking up early all the time, I did like helping our pastor with Mass and pleasing my grandmother. And part of it was probably because I received affirmations from so many people for helping out: Grandma would buy me doughnuts after Mass while I sat in the laundromat waiting for her to do her laundry, and the little old ladies at church slipped me five dollar and ten dollar bills for all sorts of occasions and would promise prayers for my well-being. I was probably the wealthiest altar server in the state of Kansas. I quickly learned how to multiply that money (buying those great packs of baseball cards with the "cardboard" bubble gum, and selling my average cards to anyone who would buy them was my earliest "business" venture, and as an altar server, I got the capital I needed to secure the goods).

I always left the church feeling content, secure in my faith, and thankful for the great people around me. I trained grade school classmates on how to serve Mass and was the de facto leader of the altar servers in my parish where I began to learn about leadership and coaching.

My parents were also instrumental in my earliest faith journeys—they were cradle-born Catholics and lived their faith as typical Catholics by never missing Mass on Sundays. No one in my family argued about going to Sunday Mass—we just did it. My mother entertained priests and religious sisters in our home with her patented steak and potatoes dinner. They knew my mother would always have a great meal prepared upon their arrival, and no one left my mother's house hungry—*never.*

I wasn't born into a family of what you might typically call "leaders." My father was a rural mail carrier for 30 years, and after he was declared legally blind in his early 50s, he worked as the supervisor of maintenance (a fancy name for a janitor) at Allen Fieldhouse at the University of Kansas until he retired at the mandatory age of 70. My father also volunteered to coach baseball for more than 30 years, had a baseball field named after him (and his brother) in Lawrence, and grew a garden each year that yielded so many vegetables my mother said we could "feed the whole county." My mother worked as a part-time secretary for various companies and a school bus driver to help pay for our family's private education. She looked after us and kept our home running.

While they both didn't necessarily achieve big, grand things, they were leaders in their own rights and were excellent examples of perseverance, grit, and, especially, selflessness. I observed them closely and learned tremendously about virtues. We didn't have extras and even though I thought we were middle class, we were, in fact, poor.

I never realized this until one day, in my early career at age 28, I had taken my father out for a meal. I was excited to tell him that I had broken the six-figure income barrier for the first time. But before I could tell him, he eagerly shared with me that he had just made the most money in a single year in his entire life. Excited, I asked him how much. He leaned over and said, with the biggest smile on his face, "Thirty-thousand dollars!"

I immediately smiled and said, "Dad, that's great! You've earned it." I was proud of him, and couldn't for the life of me tell him my news and overshadow his moment of achievement. I simply shared that I had a great year too and celebrated with him. If I remember correctly, I couldn't wrestle the lunch tab away from him as he insisted that he pay.

Maybe this is why I'm a huge subscriber to the saying, "leaders aren't born, they're made." I wasn't born into a well-off family of executives and CEOs, and in fact, I don't recall even knowing any growing up, but my parents raised me to be the leader I am today. They set an example of hard work and gave me the strength to do the same.

Apart from them, my three older brothers also tried to set an example for me, and I learned what to do, and more importantly, what *not* to do when they got in trouble. I also had a younger sister who I tried to be an exemplary role model for, so I very consciously made efforts to uphold good values and principles. This way, in my family, we all held each other accountable. Maybe this is why I'm so focused on leading by example—I understand the value of mutual respect.

My connection with my faith was always strong, even when I was a kid. So when it came time for high school, I decided to attend St Henry's Preparatory Seminary in Belleville, Illinois, to explore whether priesthood was the path for me. I left my friends in Lawrence and went into ninth grade with the philosophy of "try everything, do everything." And, phew, did I try and do *everything*—I was the editor of the high school newspaper; I helped restart the student senate and was the student senate president for two years; I played basketball and baseball; and I was even in the school plays (although, thank God, the teachers took care to make sure I was in the back of every play so I didn't embarrass myself or the rest of the cast). But something I surprisingly enjoyed was my position as a leader in our fundraising efforts for the school plays and newspaper. I was one of the top three fundraisers in every campaign and was first place by a big margin in a few of them.

I suppose that's when my passion for leadership blossomed. I liked affecting change and leading people and organizations toward positive goals. People everywhere are quick to say no. Their negativity drags you down. But I never took no for an answer, and maybe that's why I was so good at fundraising. I was never disheartened when people didn't donate—in my head, their "no" automatically translated to "not now." I would simply make the next call, and the next, and the next. I wasn't going to let a few "no"s stop me from achieving my goals.

It also helped that I had the biggest mailing list from having a large, supportive extended family. That's the only reason I can think of since I wasn't trained in this, nobody told me what to say or who to contact, and I didn't even know much about it in the first place. But I was never one to wait around and see if someone else would do it. I was competitive from an early age and hated to lose. This ability to wade through the "no"s carried me later on when I became a college admissions counselor, an assistant college baseball coach, and after that, a marketing representative in the insurance industry. Whether it was recruiting a new student or signing on a new client, I was driven to keep trying until I got the "yes" I needed to achieve my goals. And it was an *incredibly* fun challenge.

Over the years, I developed my natural talent into something that produced results by integrating strategies and doing my research. When people ask me how I achieve my fundraising goals today, I tell them that it's more than just asking people to donate; *it's an art and a science.* It's a game of persevering without letting the negativity get to you. Very few people know how to fundraise, and there are many armchair quarterbacks who love to tell you how to do it. You know the type—the guy watching football on TV, sitting in his recliner with a beer and a bag of potato chips who never played football in his life, yelling at the screen, telling Patrick Mahomes of the Kansas City Chiefs how to run the offense. These types drive me crazy and are almost always ones that never raised a dime in their lives.

One of my earliest lessons in perseverance was during my college years. I was promised an athletic scholarship prior to the start of the baseball season at Creighton University, and I was excited at the prospect because there was no way my family could afford the tuition without this scholarship—my parents didn't have the money, and I didn't have enough savings to make it through four years.

So, when I was told I could receive an athletic scholarship on top of my academic scholarship, I looked forward to starting my collegiate journey at Creighton.

But after being one of two walk-ons to make the team, the coach informed me that he no longer had any funds available to help me. I was devastated. Without the scholarship, I would not be able to afford my college education at this private Jesuit university. I had always planned to get out of school without any debt, but this wrench in my plans made it seem unlikely. When I was in the middle of figuring out what I should do, the starting catcher on the baseball team, a junior, gave me some advice that made it a lot easier to decide. He said, "Chris, I've been promised a scholarship for three years now, and I still don't have it. If you get a chance to go somewhere else and walk away, do it." And so I did.

I started looking for other schools and other scholarship programs. By divine intervention, in the form of multiple scholarship offers from St. Mary of the Plains College, the possibility of graduating debt-free didn't seem too far off. I immediately transferred at the start of the Spring semester. Even though my dream of playing NCAA Division I baseball had ended, continuing to play baseball at a small school was very appealing and exciting.

My college experience strengthened me and helped me grow as a leader—it was great all around, no regrets. I had fun, I went out to a few parties, and I had a great social life. That's the beauty of small campuses: everybody knows everybody. I mean, there was literally only one or two bars in Dodge City that we all went to; or rather, felt safe enough to venture into. Also, there were no phones or laptops then, so all you could do to pass the time was hang out with each other. I attended Mass almost every day and frequently went on Catholic retreats. In fact, my involvement with the campus ministry was what helped me stay connected to my faith.

Truthfully, I didn't need a lot of socializing to keep myself busy; I was working 20-30 hours a week through a work-study program, playing baseball, and serving as the treasurer of both the student council and the college Knights of Columbus council. Add to that attending classes and studying, and I had a pretty tight schedule.

Later on, in my junior year, I met my future wife, who was a volleyball player and just as preoccupied as I was, so I also worked hard to make sure we had time for each other. Those four years at St. Mary's were busy, but it kept me out of trouble. After all, idleness is the devil's workshop, so I dedicated myself to studying, working, playing baseball, officiating local high school football, basketball, or baseball games, and leading as much as possible. My contributions were recognized: I won a leadership award during my sophomore year (St. Thomas More Award, as voted on by the faculty), I was the homecoming king, and I was elected as Mr. Blue by the faculty and students during my senior year (which, any St. Mary's student will tell you, is quite a special leadership award).

I had baseball keeping me busy too, and it shaped me more than I thought it would. As captain of the team, I learned perseverance, endurance, and how to lead by example. My baseball career was great, but one particular event comes to mind when I think of my college baseball days: a doubleheader during my senior year.

Usually, when we played doubleheader games, we would have one of our better pitchers pitch the first game, and someone else pitch the second. As a lefthander who didn't throw very hard, I was usually chosen to pitch the second game at least once a week. So, I played the entire first game at first base, which typically lasted about three hours. This was an important game for us, and we were going full force. After three hours of intense play, our team emerged victorious in game one. We'd won! However, I couldn't take a break as we still had another game to play, and this time, *I* had to pitch.

As the second game progressed, I was pitching well, and I was having another great game at the plate, but by the seventh inning and seven hours from the start of the first game, my arms and legs were absolutely exhausted. But I was ready—I had trained myself to overcome my limits and instead focus on the next pitch, the next hitter, the next situation.

In the top of the seventh and last inning, with two outs and a one-run lead, I gave up a two-run home run to lose the lead. The head coach slowly walked out to the mound, congratulated me on a great game, and said he was going to bring in the relief pitcher. My stomach plummeted. He reassured me that I would stay in the lineup as a designated hitter to bat in the bottom of the seventh. I was a little disheartened knowing I had come this far, but I recognized it was what was best for the team. I had to put my team's best interests ahead of my own, and that was a tough pill to swallow. So, after the pitching change, my teammate threw one pitch, the hitter hit an easy pop fly to the second baseman, and we were out of the inning. One pitch, one out. It was our turn to bat.

The first batter for our team drew a walk. The coach put a pinch runner on first with me coming to the plate next. I could barely stand after being on the field for over seven hours by now but somehow found the strength to focus. After doing my typical visualization routine, I said a quick prayer and stepped into the box. I was looking for a fastball over the middle of the plate. I visualized hitting a line drive in the gap as I knew our pinch runner was fast enough to score from first and tie the game. When the pitcher finally threw it, I turned on the pitch and hit a towering flyball over the 375-foot fence in the right-field alley. As I rounded first base, the opponent's first baseman was yelling at me in colorful language—something about how I had found a way to beat them again. I smiled and slapped his hand as I passed. I was exhausted as I rounded the bases but was re-energized when all my teammates met me at home plate for a major celebration of our doubleheader sweep.

Later on, my teammate who came in to pitch in relief approached me and apologized for how he ended up getting credit as the winning pitcher, even though he only threw one pitch in contrast to the 90-odd pitches I had thrown. We laughed and understood that this is just how the game works—and it was, after all, a team effort. That's when I truly recognized and understood that as a leader, your team wins are yours as well, and every member's contributions, no matter how small, are integral to the entire team's success. I carry the same mindset of teamwork, leading in the face of adversity, and grit with me even today. A team sport can completely change your mindset that way—and even make you a better leader in the long run.

Chris playing baseball his senior year for St. Mary of the Plains College (1986) on his way to becoming the NAIA Career Batting Leader with a .480 average.

When it was time for me to leave college, I had absolutely no idea what I wanted to do. I wasn't sure what to do with the business degree I had earned. No industry pulled me in. I didn't even know what my options were. However, part of me knew what I was looking for: I enjoyed helping people achieve their full potential, reach their goals, and lead them to be the best they could be. A job that would allow me to do this would be the one for me. Once I realized this, it was easy to pick a path: I loved baseball so much that I decided to coach it.

I began as a graduate assistant and then transitioned to a full-time assistant. After all, I had already been the captain of the team, so transitioning from being a player to a coach was easy and natural. I had always led my team by my principles and setting a good example, so I knew I already had the players' respect. Plus, during my time as their captain, I had extensively studied the game and my own teammates, so I knew all of their strengths and weaknesses, which helped me come up with strategies tailored to these traits. I used to be in their shoes once, so I understood their grievances and listened to their side even while supporting the head coach—empathy is important for any leadership, and listening, as I learned, was a key part of it. I think this helped us connect better as a team, and we ended up winning the conference the first season I was the head assistant coach.

Baseball was a gift that kept giving. One, coaching has always been fun for me, and I love doing it. Two, since I've coached before—albeit in a different field and a different game (literally)—I know the landmines you need to watch out for and the work you need to do to keep progressing. I know the pressures of leading an organization, and I know what it takes to take a team from last to first. Decades later, all of this culminated in my role as an executive coach and consultant.

And it's all in the details—in baseball, I would analyze every part of my swing, and then I took the same discipline and applied it to the players and taught them how to see the finer aspects of their technique, form, and approach. This is what led me to set the NAIA career batting average at .480, which has stood since 1986. My love for teaching and coaching followed me all the way to the insurance industry where, as a marketing manager, I dove in to gather the same kind of details and analysis and help my team prepare for success and improve every day. All that observation and detail-oriented approach set me up to be an expert; I was often asked to be a guest speaker for my company's training programs. I became a mentor to other managers—they would spend time working with me and learning my secrets. It was the very core of each of my professions—as a baseball coach, regional manager, CEO, president, and founder—I applied my own formula for gaining depth and insight and coached my team on those same principles so they could be highly successful in their respective fields.

Although I loved coaching, the assistant coach position at a small school does not come with a very good paycheck, so I had to work in the admissions office as well, where I earned a whopping $16,000 for the year. I used the job to learn everything I could from those around me, including the president of the college. One day, one of my coworkers (who was also the men's basketball head coach) asked me if I had ever thought about going into insurance. And I resolutely said, "No." I wasn't even remotely interested in that field. I'd always envisioned an insurance agent as a guy in a business suit with a very short tie and enormous belly trying to sell my dad a $10,000 life insurance policy while blowing smoke from his cigarette. I never wanted to be *that* guy.

But my coworker shook his head. "No, no, no, that's not what I'm talking about. I'm talking about B2B—business to business—insurance." I had never considered this as a possibility, but the idea intrigued me. He said he knew an alum who was a marketing manager in the company and could give me a "personality" test to see if I would be a good fit. At the time, I had no clear vision of what I wanted to do in life, so I thought, "It doesn't hurt to try."

I took the test. They called me back. And after four months of interviewing, they hired me for their one-year marketing training program in the state of Minnesota, one of the finest training programs in the country.

When I look back, it seems incredible that I even started on this path, especially since I knew nothing about insurance at the time. But that's the beauty of trying everything and looking out for opportunities—they tend to work out in wonderful, unexpected ways. In some respects, my positive attitude, hard work ethic, and can-do attitude can make me feel invincible, but isn't that what success is all about?

Naysayers step aside, we are going to get the job done, no matter the obstacles that lie before us.

Learning to Lead in the Corporate World

I'd never eaten shrimp. As a poor kid growing up in Kansas, meat and potatoes were usually the meal of the day. In fact, the only time we ever ate fish was for Lent. By "fish," I mean frozen fish sticks in the oven, of course. But during my time in college, thankfully, I was exposed to a lot of new positive things, big and small, that prepared me for the future in unexpected ways.

I recall a time during my junior year in college when we were on a baseball trip in the panhandle of Oklahoma. It was a Friday during Lent, and as a Catholic, I don't eat meat on Fridays—only fish. So our coach decided to take the entire team to a restaurant with all-you-can-eat shrimp, a hungry young man's paradise! I was sitting with teammates who were from all around the country, and I told them I'd never had shrimp before. My teammates from Miami found this all very humorous and couldn't wait to see me try one. The food arrived, and we all piled the shrimp high on our plates and dug in enthusiastically. I was having a pretty good time but wasn't overly impressed with the shrimp. One of my teammates turned to me and asked, "Well? What do you think?"

I carefully assessed the mass quantities of shrimp I'd eaten and said, "I think it's good. It's different, definitely. But good." And then I added, almost as an afterthought, "It's a little crunchy though."

They all stopped eating, looked at me for a second in bewilderment, and started laughing. "You know you're supposed to peel the legs and shell off the shrimp, right?"

Peel the shrimp? I had no idea! No one had ever taught me that before. While I was frankly a little embarrassed at the time, it's rather funny to look back on. Also, thank goodness I learned my lesson in college with a bunch of baseball guys because a couple of years later, I was at a 5-star resort for a company incentive trip in Boca Raton, Florida, and you'll never guess what they served—shrimp!

It was small incidents like these that helped me grow and explore new things all the time. I owe a huge debt to my coaches at St. Mary's—they influenced my leadership style, which helped me succeed in my insurance career. They showed me that being encouraging and patient with your direct reports works a whole lot better than yelling at them. Screamers may get good short-term results, but they fail in the long run. Creating a positive and supportive environment makes people want to stay and work hard. If you have empathy for your employees and let them see you truly care about *their* success and not just your organization's bottom line, they will run through walls for you. A lot of the companies that make it to a "Top 25 Places To Work" list typically have one thing in common: an empathetic leadership style. They give their employees resources to grow and succeed, competitive pay, great benefits, and a positive, encouraging environment that keeps them happy and productive. These firms have a culture that inspires and leaders that are transformational. These firms are not transactional; *they are relational*.

A supportive environment that would help me grow was exactly what I had in mind for my career. While my coworker at St. Mary's recommended B2B insurance, I wasn't sold on it—that is, until I heard about Federated Insurance's *amazing* marketing training program. They hired a maximum of 12 people from across the country for each class, with three classes in a year. It was very competitive and just as rigorous. We started with 9 in our class, with one dropping out after 12 weeks. We were given opportunities throughout the year to apply the knowledge we had learned by taking care of customers who didn't have an agent at the moment due to retirement, promotion, or resignation. This real-life experience left me feeling well-prepared and an expert at the age of 26. We walked out of the training with a "doctorate" in commercial insurance. By witnessing the president and his cabinet fulfill their promises with integrity and respect, I gained insight into leadership values. In fact, over 50 percent of the people in my training class are either retired millionaires or are still working for the company 30+ years later. This is a great model for retention.

After that one year of phenomenal education, we were all assigned different territories. During my year-long training, as I had with all major decisions in my life, I prayed for God to give me wisdom and guidance to help me decide on a territory. This not only impacted me but also my wife and our newly-born daughter. When the offer came, I agreed to move back to Dodge City, Kansas to take over a territory of 17 counties in Southwest Kansas and the panhandle of Oklahoma. By this time, all my assumptions about insurance—the stereotypical cigarette-smoking middle-aged guy with a big belly—had completely turned around. Now, I was starting each day with tremendous knowledge not just about my field but with more insight and confidence than 90 percent of my competitors. The numerous leadership seminars I attended, and the books I read helped me gain a thorough understanding of what it takes to really *lead* and *succeed* at a high level. I was ready to transform my territory and become a top company performer.

When I first entered this territory, it was one of the worst in the company (out of 500!), but I was up for the challenge. Very few people understood what I hoped to achieve by picking a territory that was one of the worst in the company—they saw no upside. They even talked of eliminating the territory. I was convinced that I could succeed and do it in a big way. Each day, I was up early and made my first in-person call at 8 AM. There were times I would have to drive for two hours, so I would leave the house at 6 AM. I was very disciplined. Once on the road, I would say prayers for my day and then listen to motivational speakers and talks about leadership on the cassette tape player (remember those?) in my car. I immersed myself in learning my craft, and just like my college baseball career, I knew I wasn't as talented as others—but, I knew I would outwork everyone else.

When I was younger, I worked on a farm but never drove a tractor or any other equipment. So, when I was calling on farm equipment dealers in Western Kansas for my job, I knew I needed to learn about the equipment they had in their business if I wanted a leg up. So one day, I gathered the courage to ask the owner of a John Deere dealership to give me a tour. He enthusiastically said, "Yes!" As we toured, I asked him a lot of questions, including what the difference was between a tractor and a combine. He explained and then asked me if I wanted to test drive one of the $150,000 combines.

I said, "Why not?" And then, "Yes!"

So here I was, an insurance guy driving this expensive piece of machinery around the lot and loving every minute of it. A very memorable experience indeed for this kinesthetic learner.

Just as I had hoped, success came at last. After two years, we were in the top 25 of the company, and the very same people who were telling me that Dodge City was not a good territory were now telling me it was one of the best.

Shortly after, I was offered a promotion to district marketing manager in Kansas City to take over one of the worst-performing districts in the company. I relished the recognition, but as with all major decisions, I first prayed and then studied the opportunity in front of me. In leadership, you must learn not to make quick decisions on emotion if you can avoid it but know in advance what opportunities may lie ahead. I prepared my mental state for management by learning from the most successful people, picking the brains of my customers who had great knowledge of business, and taking advantage of every opportunity to give presentations to others in the company and my customers. When the opportunity arose, I was prepared to accept and start a new transition with my family, which had now grown to two daughters. I was assigned to manage eight marketing representatives, but there were only five employed, which meant I had to hire three more. I looked at this as an opportunity to build my own great team and set out to lead them to the top of the company.

Whenever you take over a group of people, you have to begin to evaluate each person to see if they can succeed and if they have the tools to help them succeed. If they didn't have the ability to succeed at this job but were great employees otherwise, I always looked for other opportunities for them within the company.

Of the people I managed in Kansas City, there was one guy in particular, "Freddie," who was a bit of a downer all the time. He was one of the most negative people you could ever meet, and nobody wanted to be around him. If it was a beautiful day, he would declare that it might rain soon. If the sun was shining and everything was great, he would complain that it was too hot. That's the kind of guy he was.

One day, when I was riding down the road with him in rural Missouri, he was telling me once again how terrible things were for him: he needs more territory, he needs more prospects, and on and on and on. I kept trying to encourage him and reinforce the good things going on with him, but he just continued to be negative.

Finally, I said, "You know, Freddie, I have some concerns. Let me ask you a few questions. Is your house paid off?"

"Yes," he said with pride.

"You have a home on the lake?" I asked.

"Yep. All paid for," he replied.

"Fantastic!" I exclaimed. "And you are in the top five percent of income earners in your hometown?"

"Oh, no doubt about that," he said.

I continued, "The company is providing you with a great deferred comp retirement plan, a wonderful 401k program, along with disability and health insurance, yes?"

He nodded. "Some of the best plans in the country."

"And your wife is driving a beautiful new Cadillac that I assume is all paid for and this car we are sitting in is very nice."

"Oh yes, everything is paid for," he continued, boasting with pride.

I hesitated for a moment and then looked him in the eye

and said, "Well, Freddie, I'm not sure we can do any better, so my question to you is: why don't you just quit?"

Freddie stepped on the brakes, pulled off on the shoulder of the road, and exclaimed, "What?!"

I repeated, "We can't do any better. All you do is complain, and I think it would be better for you to find something else to do. You're miserable. There has to be another company out there that can do better."

At that moment, something clicked for him. He didn't realize how negative he was. By helping him identify his problem and acknowledge this was a barrier to his success, I could see that I had inspired him to change his attitude and his thinking. Being a leader is about asking the hard questions at times to help employees become better versions of themselves. Freddie later told numerous people that I was the best marketing manager he ever had. Imagine that! I cared enough to call him out and help him improve—and it showed.

Leadership is about showing people the way and inspiring them to greatness. But there's a big difference between leadership and management. Management is telling people what to do, making demands you would never do yourself, and then not taking the time to teach them how to do it or give them the tools to succeed. If you are a new leader in a new position, and if you don't know much about a certain task your employees are doing, ask them to show you how they do their work or have them give a presentation to your leadership team. They will be glad to demonstrate their work for you, I guarantee it, and you can evaluate their effectiveness. This will give you great insight and the comfort to know that you have amazing people working for you.

After my direct talk with Freddie, he changed his outlook (at least around me). While occasionally he was still a little negative, he had started to approach tasks more positively and contributed a lot to the team, including presenting at team meetings. It's through that kind of one-on-one mentoring and building a connection with my employees that I was able to make a success story out of Kansas City.

Within five years, we had become one of the top-performing districts in the company. I hired one of the first women in the office and later one of the first Black employees in the whole company. I was told neither could succeed. These two individuals excelled and showed the company otherwise! Leaders find the right people, train them, and watch them grow and succeed. I didn't care if they were male or female and being in a predominantly white male company, I was seen as a bit of a rebel for hiring them but mostly as a good leader. I proved all could succeed with my leadership and the company's great training. As a manager in Kansas City, I won two major incentive trips (in addition to our annual incentive trips) including a one-week, all-expense-paid trip for my family to Orlando along with another all-expense-paid 15-day, 6-star cruise on the Mediterranean, from Rome to London, with our CEO and his wife. I was asked to share my success with other new managers and spoke frequently at company meetings and training seminars. I was building a track record of going into the worst places and turning them around.

In the fall of 1999, Federated asked me to transfer, to duplicate what I had been doing and help them build a new district in Southern California. This would be a major challenge. My wife had previously told me that she was willing to move anywhere *but* California. We now had four children and moving was becoming more and more difficult. Like every major decision, I took it to prayer, studied the opportunity, and wrote down all the positives and negatives if I were to accept.

I listened to those in upper-level management who were successful and had long, intense discussions with my wife. In my prayer, I asked the Lord many times, "Why California?" Why couldn't I be offered an opportunity that was a well-oiled machine in Texas or Florida? So far, everything I had prayed for had happened with numerous miracles and more. I was blown away that everything I asked for was given to me, and so I accepted the opportunity. My territory would eventually span from LA to San Francisco and everything in between—a great market with lots of potential but a little overwhelming. When I started, there were four people on my team, which meant we all had to take on a lot of responsibilities, and I was solely responsible to hire more people quickly for the remaining six territories.

I enjoyed coaching my marketing representatives, and eventually, my marketing managers. I found that sometimes when an employee is struggling, being empathetic and finding solutions with them can usually lead to an easy fix. Other times, some need a little more coaching than others and one of my employees in LA comes to mind.

I inherited this young, new marketing representative in LA who had very little training. He was failing miserably. I tried to help him and came up with a plan for him, but after a short time working with him, I would show up at his place, and he would still be sleeping. He was a partier and a little bit of a playboy. I saw potential in him, and I knew he could succeed, but he needed to get his act together.

It was time to grow up, leave his college ways behind, and become a professional. After waking him up twice upon my arrival at his apartment to begin the work day, I gave him an ultimatum: 30 days to pull it together and make a change, or I was going to make a change.

But I didn't just threaten him, set him at the edge of a cliff, and leave him there. I sat down with him, came up with an action plan, and told him I would hold him accountable every week. I showed him that he had a goldmine in the city of LA, and if he would just listen to my plan, he could lead the company in sales. He was young and inexperienced, and honestly, I think he probably was afraid and intimidated at the thought of calling on business owners twice his age. I wanted to push him, but I didn't have time to hold his hand either. I showed him the way to success by putting together a very specific action plan with his input and then following up each week, and I offered my support—he could call me anytime for anything, and I would find a way to help him and get him the resources he needed.

This is coaching; I was patient, I saw potential, and I helped him live up to it. He was fresh out of college and had no direction, but he was honest; all he needed was a little leadership and someone to believe in him. I knew he could make it; he was a fun guy, good-looking, smart, and everybody who met him liked him. He needed structure, and I gave him that. Each week we reconvened, planned out the weeks according to what we thought was reasonable to expect from him, and I put trust in him to take it from there. He called with minor and major successes. He was excited, and I joined him in his enthusiasm.

Later on, he told me that initially he was really mad at me and complained to his dad about me. I asked him what his dad said, and he told me all his dad said was to be thankful he had a boss who cared. I admired his dad because of this. He could have easily joined in the complaint, but he cared, just like I did. To make a long story short, he ended up leading the company in proposals for the year and was in the top ten of sales. Talk about a complete 180! He thanked me numerous times for challenging and believing in him like no one had done before. They had simply accepted his lackluster effort, but when I showed I cared, he succeeded.

This is why I loved openly communicating with my direct reports about their needs and their plans to succeed. Being empathetic can have a long-lasting, positive effect. Some people might respond to a more strict, overbearing style where managers yell and threaten their employees and create an overall environment that is unbearably high pressure. But honestly, that's never worked for me. I mean, who wants to work under the veil of a threat all the time or not know where the finish line is? What does success look like?

I have found most managers who threaten were rarely successful on their own. Jobs are hard enough; no one needs the extra pressure. What a lot of managers don't understand is that employees have a life other than just work, and oftentimes, you can never tell when someone is going through something in their personal life or what they're lacking. The job of a good leader is to figure out what they need and give them those resources to succeed. Just asking a simple question—"How can I help?"—can go a long way.

I had an awesome manager who revealed the secret to exceptional leadership: hire great people and you will be successful. As I state in numerous conversations about leadership, "High tide raises all ships." As a leader, you can't do the work for your people; you must train them, mentor them, and then get out of their way to allow their (and your) success to blossom. When I got started in California, the work to hire was daunting because not only did I have to work with the people I already had, but I also had to do all human resources work like putting ads in the newspapers (Indeed and LinkedIn were not well-known then), completing a series of eight interviews on every candidate, networking, and building the territory.

The area of California that I lived in still had dial-up internet at the time, which made connectivity a challenge. I had an analog cell phone plan that only had 60 minutes of talk time. I had to go to the library to do market research for all areas and was excited to find a company that sold the yellow pages on a floppy disc with information about potential prospects. If you lived in this era, you remember. I didn't know any different. I just moved and worked hard and prayed my efforts would be successful. I knew my success wasn't about me; it was an opportunity that the Lord put in my path and He would not allow me to fail. I was comforted by this thought and plowed forward. All the hard work paid off and within three years of starting up this expansion territory, my district became the #1 district in the company in numerous categories, and I earned the top management award in the company: the Achievement of Excellence Award.

My train of success kept rolling: I was asked once again to take over another challenging area of the country and with prayer, I accepted a promotion to regional marketing manager in Kentucky where I took over a five-state region, and led a team of 70 marketing people, overseeing approximately $90-100 million in insurance premiums. Moving my family with five children now seemed easier since we were going back to our midwestern roots, but it was going to take a lot of work for another turnaround by leading four managers (out of six) with less than one year of experience.

The region lacked leadership, but I saw great potential in the managers I was going to lead. During my experiences there, I realized that what the marketing people really needed from me was positive affirmations, as my predecessor was not one to hand out compliments freely. I wanted everyone to realize that they were valuable to the organization. In their line of business, the word "no" was what they heard most often. If their manager was just another person giving them negativity, then their productivity and self-confidence were bound to sink. My method was working so well because I led by example, and I led with a positive outlook. If someone said, "no," I would tell them they were just one step closer to a "yes."

I was now working with mid-level managers and helping them be successful. I helped them spot the opportunities and gave them the tools to succeed. As a regional manager, I implemented accountability strategies while also being empathetic to my direct reports. I made sure to ask—"What do you need?" "What's holding you back?" "How can I help?"—rather than assume they're not putting in the effort. At least two times a month, I would travel to their area to work with them in the field and do things they didn't particularly enjoy. We'd laugh at our failures and celebrate their successes. When you get out and see customers, you get a sense of the performance of your employee and receive valuable feedback. Every leader knows how crucial this is.

This also boosted morale because they saw me as someone willing to get "in the trenches" and see their world. I also took their spouses out to dinner and got to know their families as well. Building relationships with your people is a critical component of leadership as it allows you to get to know them better. I wanted to show that I cared about more than just results—I was also deeply invested in my employees themselves.

I had picked up a lot about leadership during my time at Federated and wanted to branch out on my own and try my entrepreneurial skills. I was also traveling frequently, almost three to four nights a week, and it was taking a toll on my young family and me. My wife had quit her job as a schoolteacher when I joined Federated Insurance in 1989 and had stayed home to look after our children. She didn't enjoy moving frequently, which came with each promotion, but her faith was strong, and she supported me through prayer and as a confidant in my work. I couldn't have done it without her, and I definitely would've never been able to jump into opportunities if she wasn't there to hold down the fort at home, especially with five children in 2003. We were also blessed to find supportive communities everywhere we went. I often joked that my kids were "corporate brats" (like the affectionate military term) because we kept moving around so much, but I also reinforced that they had friends all over the country because of these moves. I often referred to our time in California as a three-year vacation!

When we moved to a new city, the first thing we would look for was the local Catholic church. Since our kids were homeschooled at the time, we always found a homeschool group so our kids could engage and connect. In Kentucky especially, the homeschool support was *big* as they had a large homeschool co-op where all the kids would come together one to two days a week and certain parents would teach a class or two to help out other parents. They had a homeschool sports team, and the kids played travel soccer and travel basketball and even did some fine arts stuff. So the kids had a whole network of friends. I wanted to coach my sons' baseball teams and my daughters' basketball teams. My travel schedule had prevented me from doing this before.

So with a lot of prayer, I decided to step away from a very successful and lucrative insurance career and take an opportunity to invest, own, and run a healthcare company. I wanted to test my leadership skills and see how I would fare as the owner of a company. I agreed to become the Chief Operating Officer and take over two struggling hospice programs and help turn these two companies around. But I also wanted to stay home more so I could spend time with my family; I wanted more flexibility, and I wanted to lead from the top. But the timing wasn't good, the promises made to me were not fulfilled, and the financials were much worse than proposed. I wish I spent more time studying the inner workings of this industry like I did with insurance, but I allowed my personal desires to get in the way. Within a year, and after increasing the size of the programs by over 50 percent, I realized that it just wasn't going to work out. I decided to cut my losses and take this as a lesson I needed to learn. As an entrepreneur, you take calculated risks, and sometimes they don't work out.

You've got to be careful getting into an industry you don't know much about. For example, if I had bought an insurance brokerage instead, I would've probably been a lot more successful since I had abundant knowledge in that field. Additionally, having a team to support you and do the legwork also helps—that way, they can fill in the gaps in information for you. My healthcare business suffered because I didn't have a thorough understanding of what it entailed, but boy, did I pay a heavy price for this education. I managed to change policies and procedures, and we increased our patients substantially but that growth brought in a lot of challenges that I wasn't prepared for. I learned a lot about Medicare reimbursements during this time and have to say, I probably learned more about this than most because it was my own investment that was at risk. After all of this, I was ready to head back into my industry of expertise—insurance.

While on a silent retreat in Southwestern Ohio where I was praying about my future, I met a great man who shared my passion for insurance and owned a large insurance brokerage. I found this meeting kind of ironic since I managed to hit it off with him in a place where we weren't allowed to talk. We agreed to meet up later to discuss opportunities with his company. I asked him if he had a place for me in his Lexington, KY office. We quickly reached an agreement, and I started working for him in 2006.

Getting back into commercial insurance was as easy as riding a bike. I didn't have a book of business but did have a lot of networking contacts—my friend's company definitely took a bit of a risk with me. All I said was, "Give me a salary, a computer, and a phone, and I'll go to work, and I will make up the salary to you within one year." After six months, I accomplished the aggressive goal by "making up my salary" in revenue, which solidified our relationship.

It was just one of those instances when all your previous experiences play into your success, and all I did was put my leadership principles in place and do what I do best. They gave me great support and treated all of their employees extremely well. Soon, I was seen as a leader in the office. But while I supported the leadership that was already in place, I wasn't officially in charge of managing anyone, which gave me a lot of freedom and flexibility, and I really enjoyed my time there, especially when our seventh child arrived shortly after in late 2008.

During my time in Lexington, I was also involved with my church and focused a lot of my energy on giving back to my church and the community. I supported many small non-profit organizations and tried to help out as much as I could. I was on the executive committee for our baseball league and did a lot of fundraising (our team had the best uniforms and equipment!) as well as coached my sons' baseball and basketball teams. Apart from that, I was also involved in a Catholic-based virtue program for young men, 5 to 15-year-olds, where a group of dads met once a week to mentor our young sons and other young men who didn't have a father figure in their home. I set up a non-profit and raised funding for a homeschool basketball team that traveled, playing teams across the Midwest. I didn't really think much about these volunteer opportunities, but I was enjoying it. It was just my way of giving back to my community and engaging with my church, and it was a great way to share my leadership skills with others outside of the corporate environment.

But that's not all—this also rekindled my passion for doing something bigger than myself. I enjoyed insurance and had a lot of success once again, but I just didn't feel a mission-driven purpose at the brokerage. It was a great job, and I made a lot of money, but I wanted to do more for my community and my church. So I started looking for places where I could apply my skills and *really make a difference.*

My chance to lead something big came in the form of a higher education career, and in October 2012, I jumped in.

The Higher
Education
Calling

I was reading a Catholic newspaper in an airport in Texas as I was waiting to board a connecting flight to California for one of my incentive trips, when I saw an ad for a position at Franciscan University in Steubenville, Ohio. They were looking for an executive director for their 25+ high school youth and adult conferences across the United States and Canada that they hold every summer. Franciscan has a great youth ministry program where young people are transformed over the course of a weekend conference. I had read a lot about Franciscan University of Steubenville thanks to Dr. Scott Hahn, who is on the faculty. He is a brilliant theologian, an international speaker, and a well-accomplished author. I'd read many of his works, listened to his talks, and was deeply impressed by him, and through his books, I got a glimpse of Franciscan University. I found that it was a Catholic institution congruent with many of my own philosophies and ideals, and it was high on my list of great Catholic universities. They had a great mission.

I had limited experience in youth ministry, but I did know how to run organizations. On a whim, I thought, *I'm looking for something different, and I've heard a lot of great things about the University. Why not apply and see what happens?* I prayed about this and decided to send them my resume and went back to work.

To my surprise, I got a call back within a week and after a couple of interviews, I was a finalist. Ultimately I didn't get the job, but I wasn't too heartbroken over it—it would have been a major pay cut, after all. I submitted to God's will as this was one of the first jobs I applied for that I didn't get. But I also realized that somebody better than me got the job; perhaps they had a skill set I did not have. So I just accepted my fate and put that to rest.

A couple of weeks later, the university called me back and told me they were creating a new position and were looking for someone to build their Major Gift division—would I be interested? Well, I had some experience with fundraising that would be an asset, and I was looking to lead and develop something big. I'd worked in a higher education setting before as a college baseball coach and admissions counselor prior to my insurance career and I had thoroughly enjoyed that environment. Plus, by then I'd realized that to move up in the higher education field, I needed an advanced degree, especially because I was aiming for executive leadership positions within the university. Here an opportunity had presented itself where I could work and get my MBA at the same time. So, in October 2012, I made the move to Steubenville and started at Franciscan as the Director of the Major Gifts and, shortly after, enrolled in their MBA program.

After working for a few months, I realized that this was a *major* paradigm shift. In the corporate world, you're moving and running constantly and there's only one speed—*fast*. People take risks, and if it doesn't work out, they just find a way to course-correct and move forward. But in the university setting, it was the complete opposite. There were many different factions involved in the decision-making processes which really slowed down the pace. Getting everyone's opinion and carefully thinking through each decision isn't a bad way to do things, but it was something I needed time to get used to.

I experienced this when I tried to execute my first task: fundraising for a new fieldhouse expansion for the athletic department. It was a fairly new athletic department, and I was excited to be working with the athletic director to raise $500,000 to get started on a new fitness center. I was still new to the process, but I soon found out that while on paper I only had to work with the athletic director, in reality, I needed the green light from many other departments. Since this was a financial project, I needed to include the finance operations people as well as get approval from the President and Board; and since I would be making major presentations, I needed to coordinate with the marketing and communications department to help me with the creative assets. I jumped through a lot of hoops and the many logistics to coordinate everything slowed down the process, but ultimately, we managed to raise more than what we needed within twelve months—we had a million dollars!

It was a successful endeavor, but it really opened my eyes to the higher education industry. My day-to-day involved meetings with donors, working with a team to research each of our potential donors and come up with a plan, and finding new, creative, and impactful ways to fundraise. I studied; I attended conferences; I talked to some of the best. I hired a great team around me and began training them, much like I did in my previous career. There's a lot more to fundraising than just asking for money; there's tons of research involved which is crucial to making the ask. The data is the science behind it. On the other hand, a crucial aspect of fundraising is figuring out how you're going to pose the question, inspire donors, and involve them in the mission—that's where the "art" comes in.

You want to match your ask with their interests—just because they have money doesn't mean they're willing to give to your cause. I learned this fallacy early. Many people who have never been involved in fundraising think that you just need to ask your wealthy friends for money and they will give. Not so fast. You have to match their personal philosophies, gain their trust, and build their curiosity. The higher their interest in your mission and the ability for them to see and believe in your vision, the higher their involvement and the more they will be inspired to donate to your great cause. During my time as Director of Major Gifts, I raised funds for a lot of causes: departmental projects, research funds and grants for professors, a new capital campaign, and many more. I was involved with almost every department in the university in some capacity, including traveling with the president and the chancellor.

But while my professional life was going through a complete shift from the corporate industry to higher education, in my personal life, my family and I were coping with a difficult tragedy. In April 2013, right after we moved to Ohio, our son, who was seven and a half months along, was stillborn. It was very painful and unbelievable—I vividly remember holding him in my hands when he was delivered, but he had already found his place in heaven. God called him home early.

As a father, my goal is to lead all my kids into heaven, and I know he's waiting there for us already. My son's mortal life was brief, but he didn't have to endure all the trials, sufferings, and tragedies of this world. We tried to put a positive spin even in the midst of grieving, but it wasn't easy. Every person in the family grieved differently. My late wife was understandably going through a lot, but we all found our strength together through prayer and looked to the Lord to help us through it. I don't know how else to explain it, but a kind of supernatural grace fell upon me. It was the only way my family and I could've received the strength to persevere.

Our community and the university supported us through this. They brought us meals for eight weeks straight and helped us through a very tough time. During all this, I was still walking that tightrope, continuing my work at the university, and supporting my grieving family at home. At the time we actually had a small farm with chickens, horses, dogs, and cats, and a large garden. So I tried to get my family together, taking care of our small "farm," walking through the woods, and spending time outdoors. We kept ourselves busy and occupied, and tried our best not to dwell on the tragedy.

I was able to spend a lot of these healing moments with my family thanks to the compassionate leadership at Franciscan. In fact, it taught me a lot about how important it is for leaders to be empathetic, and the difference it can make in people's lives, which typically goes unnoticed. The university told me to take all the time I needed to help my family. It was not just an empty offer—they meant it and made sure I followed through. I saw that their leadership was beyond empathetic, it was transformational. All the leadership skills I admired and used as a leader came back as a gift to me.

When leaders of any organization put that kind of trust in you to take care of your personal life, you become more inspired and motivated to work harder for an organization because you know they *care*. And truly, it's the embodiment of what Teddy Roosevelt said: "They don't care about how much you know until they know how much you care." Boasting about your accomplishments or your credentials will not make you a good leader, nor will people even care about how much knowledge you have. But if you're empathetic and compassionate, your insights and teachings come through. This has been true for me in almost every leadership position I have undertaken, and I live by it. Because I've had empathetic employers, I was able to experience first-hand the gratitude I felt toward them and the people I worked with. It took away a lot of the stress of the job. This was one more reminder that the empathic leadership style I had been practicing since my baseball coach days had been meaningful and impactful. Ultimately, this leads to transformational leadership.

While I was going through this personal tragedy and getting used to my new position at the university, I was also earning my MBA. Balancing all of this was not the easiest thing I'd ever done. It took a lot of discipline. Most of my classes were in the evenings, and a few were online. So I found ways to work around my work schedule and take all the classes I needed. I was so busy during this time that it reminded me of my 18-credit semesters at St. Mary's. I didn't waste time because I had no time to waste. I was working 60 hours a week and had to be a leader at my workplace; I had to focus on my family, especially after our loss. In the midst of these responsibilities, I needed to study and prepare for my exams and finish assignments. I was very busy and so had to be very focused—which was not a bad thing. I compartmentalized everything and allocated time: two hours to prepare for my studies, four hours to prepare for work, and so on.

Once I finished my MBA in 2015 with the top leadership award for the class, the business department chair asked if I would want to work as an adjunct professor in marketing. I *loved* marketing, and I loved teaching and presenting as it is one of my strengths, so of course I said yes. I taught a couple of semesters and I enjoyed every aspect of it. In fact, teaching reminded me of coaching and it's surprising how closely they're related. I had a lot of fun with the students, and to be honest, I think they probably loved my class as well since I wasn't a strict grader. Who doesn't like an easy A class? As an adjunct, I didn't want to traumatize the kids by making them work unreasonably hard for their grades—it was an entry-level marketing class and I wanted them to have fun, learn, and actually get interested in the subject and possibly major in business. I could see that my students did end up enjoying the class and many are now doing great things and still are in touch with me.

But my time as an adjunct professor and director of major gifts was marked by another personal tragedy. In August 2015, my wife was diagnosed with late-stage III breast cancer. It was a completely different type of tragedy than losing one's child. When my wife was battling cancer, I was in operations mode: I was making plans and making sure she made all the doctor's and chemo appointments, that she was getting the treatment she needed and the right medications, and taking her back and forth from hospitals. I was juggling my work and family once again. I prayed every day for our Lord's help and trusted everything would be okay. I thought to myself that there was no way I could raise seven kids on my own, so I chose not to entertain the thought and focus on her healing and recovery.

My wife, on the other hand, was in survival mode: all she could think about was not dying. When you're battling something like cancer, it's hard for your mind to think clearly. The big 'C' brings a lot of anxiety, and I knew she needed my support. So I was an advocate, trying to help her navigate everything and make sure she got everything she needed. I never missed a single one of her doctor appointments.

At that time, I was a leader at work and a professor, and I had to keep working through it. Once again my employer and the leadership at the time gave me all the support and resources that they could: I was reminded again of how each person, an employee or a leader or a student, carries with them personal tragedies that may or may not be public. Thankfully, Franciscan University was in sync with my own personal ideals and leadership styles, and I'm thankful for the community that helped us through another tragedy. In fact, I actually worked harder for them and raised more money than the goals I set forth because I was so appreciative of their support.

At home, it was tough to transition from being a workplace leader to a compassionate father. Kids are not impressed by your titles or what you do. Not to mention, my children were putting up with more than just their mom's illness and the loss of a sibling—they needed to deal with school, their own work, social media pressures, and other situations we, as parents, weren't even aware of. So, when I came home for the day, I was very conscious of making that mental transition from Business Leader to Father. I knew my kids didn't need me to tell them what to do, but rather to support and encourage them.

It's definitely not easy, however, and there were numerous times when I was exasperated and exhausted. I asked the Lord for strength every day and gathered our family for prayer every day. Carrying your work home is not fair to them, and it's very easy to slip and forget that they have lives of their own (just like how certain employers forget that their employees have lives other than work). Kids need their parents and if the stresses of work carry over to the home, it creates a chaotic environment and not a safe haven, like all of us need. You must bring a different style of leadership home.

My family in 2015 (minus my oldest daughter) one week prior to my late wife's cancer diagnosis.

One of the things that helped ground me when I was walking on the leadership tightrope was my faith. The heavy winds of life can sometimes blow you off the "tightrope" of life, which means you have to focus. I never quit going to daily Mass, no matter what life threw at me. My faith and prayer life were strong, and it, in turn, gave me the strength to keep moving forward. One step at a time. A tightrope walker focuses on their feet . . . one step in front of the other. You can't always identify it, but for me, the grace that comes from prayer and the solitude it brings helps clear my vision. When you're in the midst of noise all the time, it's hard to hear and listen to where God is calling you, or for that matter, any other decisions you need to make. It's hard to think. It's hard to find strength. But in the silence of my prayer, I could think ahead, make plans, and gain insight into how I can be a better leader—both at home and at work. I had to be precise in everything I did and make sure we came to a successful conclusion with my wife's cancer battle. Praise God, after a nine-month battle, she was declared cancer-free.

As my family and I were getting used to calmer waters at home after the cancer battle, I had no intention of changing jobs anytime soon. I liked my job at Franciscan, after all. However, the one exception I made was if any offer came along for a C-suite level position at a university or other non-profit. I wasn't actively looking for anything, but I suppose I was manifesting it when I said I was open to looking.

A year after my wife's cancer-free diagnosis, I was calling on a donor in Kansas City who asked if I would be interested in getting back to the area where I grew up. All I said was, "Sure. For the right opportunity." He asked me to clarify, and I said I was only interested if it was a cabinet-level leadership position, like a CEO or a President. And he came back at me with: "I just had breakfast with our bishop, and he's looking for a new CEO of Catholic Charities in Kansas City. Would you mind if I put your name in?"

What were the odds?! I agreed immediately. My favorite aspect of any job is leadership and watching people succeed at high levels, and here I would have a wonderful opportunity to work with an organization that was in tandem with my own mission in life: serving the poor and vulnerable. Within a few hours, the bishop called me and we talked at length about the position. I took it to prayer, and six weeks later, I got a callback.

My family and I put our house up for sale and packed our bags. We were moving to Kansas City, Missouri.

I was going to start a new chapter in my career as the CEO of Catholic Charities of Kansas City-St. Joseph.

CHAPTER
FOUR

Giving Back

I've always told my kids: "Home is where the heart is."

Every time we moved to a new place in a new city, this philosophy rang true. I was blessed that my mom lived in the same house for 62 years and even now, when I visit, I can go back and sleep in the same room that I did as a little boy. While my kids didn't get to experience this tradition, I tried to help them understand that "home" didn't have to be a physical place—it could be us, a family. We were always together, and we knew we could rely on each other. The house, the neighborhood, the schools, and the workplace may have changed multiple times over many years, but we always had our family.

When we moved to Kansas City, we settled in quickly. I was beyond energized to start my new job as a CEO. I had been waiting for this opportunity; being able to lead a faith-based organization, especially one that was giving back to the community, was an incredible blessing.

Unlike my shift from insurance to higher education, getting started in a non-profit organization was an easier transition professionally. My earlier experience with fundraising and education came in handy. I had to create revenue streams and find ways to raise money to stabilize and build out our organization. Catholic Charities of Kansas City-St. Joseph had struggled financially for years and, as many non-profits experience, they weren't sure on how to create revenue streams other than the traditional model of grants and donations. I brought in the discipline and principles I had learned over my years in the insurance industry and higher education, and led with the same empathy that I had both practiced and received.

One of my principles as a leader was to create a vision for a mission that everyone in the organization could rally around. When I first came to Catholic Charities, it took me one look to pinpoint what was lacking—the mission itself. Employees didn't understand the mission, and the culture of the organization reflected this. They all had a heart to serve people in great need, but as I shared with my staff, so do numerous other non-profits working in this segment. I challenged them by asking, "What makes us different?" And, "Why would people want to donate to Catholic Charities versus the other 32,000 non-profits in the state of Missouri?"

The looks of bewilderment in the employees' eyes were stark—they really didn't have an answer. So my first challenge was to establish a clear vision. I read books of other great leaders and pulled scripture passages to help me convey the proper message. I read St. (Pope) John Paul II's and St. (Mother) Teresa of Calcutta's writings on serving the poor. I began to see a clear, consistent message that resonated with our mission and at that point, I began to repeat it again and again and again:

"We're here to serve. We're here to serve and to lift every person we meet. We're here to serve those that come to our door every day. We're here to serve people where they are & to lift them to the dignity of self-reliance."

I ensured that every single employee knew exactly who we were. We weren't just another charitable organization; we were a charitable organization that was laser-focused on serving people and empowering them. Our purpose was very specific.

It's so important that as a leader you don't water down the message. Leaders want to pontificate and show how smart they are by giving lengthy quotes or creating mission statements that are long and boring. You have to be short and concise with your messaging or you will lose the interest of the vast majority of people. Let's face it, people today get most of their information from short messages on their phone or social media outlets. Very few are willing to read lengthy articles, letters, or books. Do you realize that your employees receive an average of 100-125 business emails every day? As executive leaders, we know we receive two to three times this amount. According to numerous sources, the average person spends more than two hours on social media every day, while the average American checks their mobile devices 159 times per day. In addition to social media, people spend time on other things online and a recent statistic showed that Americans spend more than 6 ½ hours per day online.[1]

Knowing this and knowing our employees have lives outside of work, leaders must keep their messages short, clear, and concise or you will never get your vision and mission statements through to them. This isn't to say you can't give a lengthy explanation up front to explain your vision, but once described, you must repeat it in a short, concise way. Sometimes, institutions tend to have a paragraph or a page-long mission statement and ultimately it collects dust on the shelf. No one takes the time to read it. I have offended many scholars who believe you need to detail your mission statement further, but times have changed. The vast majority of people won't read it and they won't get behind it. I firmly believe that if your mission statement is more than a sentence or two, is it *really* a mission *statement?*

So, I sat down with my VP of Marketing, Kevin Murphy, and we came up with a motto to reflect our ultimate mission—"To serve people where they are and to lift them to the dignity of self-reliance"—and simply made our tagline, "To serve and to lift." Everyone understood this message and ultimately, we rebranded the whole organization around this mission statement. Kevin did an awesome job of spending hours with employees communicating and explaining the message. It became the driving force behind everything we did as an organization. Every talk I gave, to employees, benefactors, the public, I recited the phrase, "To serve and to lift," and everyone immediately grasped exactly what our mission was.

Old

New

Kevin Murphy, our VP of Marketing, noticed that while most Catholic Charities used the traditional logo, the best ones were those that did not. So we decided to completely rebrand. He and his team redesigned the logo to include the gold-domed downtown cathedral and the cityscapes of Kansas City & St. Joseph, and the tagline, "To Serve and To Lift." We later included this beautiful logo in all of our branding—envelopes, thank you cards, podcasts, and even on a bandaid dispenser!

Having a mission statement is incredibly important, no matter the industry. In the nonprofit world, if you don't have a mission that people can get behind, they have no incentive to give to your cause. In the corporate world, stockholders will not purchase your stock unless they can see a clear path to profitability. In other words: *no mission, no money.* It's a necessity. If you want to cultivate a culture and an identity in your organization, the mission is your backbone.

In fact, I found that it's also an effective screening tool. In order to make transformational culture happen, you have to know the people you're working with and who is working for you, especially those on the front lines of your organization. This is why when I started at Catholic Charities, I personally interviewed every single candidate who came through the door. I would ask them if they understood the purpose of the organization and if they believed in or could appreciate our mission. I would lay the vision and mission statement down in front of them during the interview and ask them to read it and then sit quietly. Once they had read it, I would ask them, "Do you have any questions or concerns with this? Can you envision yourself working for this cause? "

If they don't get the mission, it's problematic in the long run. I had a person once who had a great resume who told me, "I don't believe in God" when the mission statement clearly defined we were at the service of Jesus Christ. I would ask the candidate if talking about God every day would be an issue for them and if they hesitated and appeared to just want a job versus joining us for our mission, it raised red flags for me. Articulating our mission helped me find people who aligned with our values, and I was able to filter out those who may have not been the right fit for their sake and our organization. As a leader, many times you are under pressure to fill a position quickly and feel like you can't afford to turn people away; but the biggest mistake you can make is rushing to a decision and "settling" on a candidate to fill a position. If you are trying to change the culture and hire for the mission, you must be patient. If you don't do this, you will be looking for a new replacement within a year or two and the frustrations continue.

Hiring to the mission connects you with great people. I found my VP of Marketing, Kevin Murphy, through this process. He had decided to put all of his skills in marketing and communication for the Church—he had felt the same unfulfillment as I had in my previous roles. When I told him about the mission of Catholic Charities, he saw the sincerity and the faith behind it, and it got him onboard to work with us. He had seen that in the Catholic world, marketing was never much appreciated. But I could see that marketing was *everything*, especially with how Catholic Charities hadn't progressed before I got behind the wheel. So I assured him that in this organization, his skills would be put to good use and appreciated. Changing a culture takes time, and that change starts with one person at a time and it starts with you as the leader.

Changing culture takes *guts*. As a leader, you need to make bold decisions and only then can you affect change. When I started with Catholic Charities, it was in a tough situation. There were major financial challenges and most people I talked to didn't want to be involved with us because, as one donor put it, "Your organization is neither Catholic nor charitable." Ouch! I never forgot this. So as CEO, I knew I had to turnaround not just the financials, but also the culture and the public perception.

When I arrived, our offices were in a huge three-story building in downtown Kansas City. There were very few displays of the Catholic faith in the building that would signify that this was a Catholic organization. I mean, usually when you enter a Catholic church or a Buddhist temple or a Jewish synagogue, you can immediately identify their faith by the symbols, statues, windows, candles, and other items that reflect their beliefs. For example, in a Catholic church, you can usually identify the church as being Catholic when you see a crucifix on the wall, stained glass windows that might tell the story of Christ's life, or figurines of saints and martyrs. But in our huge office building, not only was there empty space everywhere, but there were very few signs of Catholicism. In fact, if the sign in the front didn't say "Catholic Charities of Kansas City-St. Joseph," you may never have even known!

The good news was that the interim CEO had started the process of selling the building and I was very supportive of this decision. Within my first month, I signed the contract to sell and move to a new location. We needed to be closer to the people we served in the inner city and selling the building not only relieved a lot of debt, but it also created new opportunities for growth.

I made sure that everything about our new office was completely revamped. My vision was to turn our new building into one that captured the very ethos of who we were. There are 32,000 nonprofits in the state of Missouri. *What made Catholic Charities different? Why should people want to give to us and not to the other 32,000 nonprofits?* Nobody knew. So, I concluded, a complete rebranding was long overdue.

In our new building, the first thing I did was put a chapel in the front of the office. I named all the rooms after saints who served the poor as it was a way to not only honor the people who lived great lives of holiness and service, but also to inspire us, as an organization, to learn from them and follow in their footsteps. I stenciled quotes by Mother Teresa and St. John Paul II on the walls. When people walked in, they immediately knew we were a Catholic organization and we welcomed them as if they were Christ himself. It was a total change of culture.

And just like every leader who tries to change things up, I received a lot of negative feedback. I was told that because of this rebranding, we could stand to lose all of our non-Catholic donors. I understood this sentiment, but I highly doubted that would be the case. I researched our database and learned that there were very few donors of other faith beliefs. As a leader, you can't always trust what people tell you and you must conduct your own research, especially if they are just giving you their subjective opinion.

When I completed my donor research and moved forward with my vision, my hunch was right—our donations actually increased! Once our Catholic donors saw the change in the rebranding of the organization, they had a renewed sense of faith and confidence in our mission. On the other hand, our non-Catholic donors kept giving because they supported our mission to serve those in need. And these donations helped us expand our reach and multiply the services we provided.

The changes I made weren't limited to just outward expressions or physical transformations—I also worked hard to shift the culture within our organization. I had an open-door policy with employees and welcomed them to come and talk to me anytime. A lot of people did come in with great questions that helped smooth the changes I was implementing. One particular employee was an ordained minister of her own church in the inner city of Kansas City and my changes inspired questions from her. We had great discussions about each other's faith, beliefs, our churches, and through our dialogue and her help, I created a new sense of trust between me and the employees. She became an advocate and was a beautiful witness to our ministry. Many times, we would just sit over the lunch hour discussing religious matters. It was enlightening.

This transformational change I spearheaded was aimed at turning a cold environment into a warm, inviting one, shifting our interactions with each other from transactional to relational. Sure, you can keep crunching numbers all day, get the grants you need, and convince people you are serving the poor population, but that doesn't *really* serve the people who are in great need. Where's the human element in numbers? When you're involved in a service-related industry, spending time with every person who walks through the door is important, whether it's just greeting them with a smile at your door, talking to them for 30 minutes, or praying with them. After all, every person is created by God in His own image, and are therefore beautiful—but some of them have harder lives and very difficult personal circumstances that they didn't necessarily create on their own. While we could provide food and basic necessities, what more could we do? More importantly, what could we do *differently*?

We established the Welcome Center where we interviewed and talked to people about their lives and current situation. After learning more about their circumstances, we tried to funnel them into one of our programs where we could best serve them. If they needed their electric bill paid or housing, we helped them find places they could afford; if they were unemployed, we helped them build their resumes and used our contacts with different employers to find a job; if they didn't have the necessary skills, we enrolled them in one of our many training programs; if there was a homeless or low-income mother that needed help, we had a family services program to help educate them about proper nutrition and how to care for their children. I asked my employees to turn their focus to creating a holistic difference by helping vulnerable people with their physical *and* spiritual needs. We were going above and beyond in carrying out our mission and living our faith.

I started up many programs at Catholic Charities to better serve the people in our area. We had 27 counties in rural Missouri and they desperately needed us as some lived in the poorest counties in the state. But because they were spread across such a wide area, there was no way we could help them out from two office locations (we had a second office in St. Joseph, MO). The poor who needed help couldn't afford to come to us either because gas was too expensive or other transportation was a major problem. So we created a mobile unit to go to *them* instead with the idea that we could provide the same service our office provided, but in a mobile unit. I wanted to bring not just help, but also hope.

During my two and a half years with the organization, we also received $6.5M in funding to build a new 38 unit low-income senior housing complex in St. Joseph, MO. It was a beautiful complex and provided much needed affordable housing for one of our most in-need and often overlooked segments of the population.

One of the most important things we did was organize a massive project that provided transitional housing for women who were homeless, vulnerable, and in great need. Because poverty was so abundant in Missouri, many women were in very difficult situations where they could not see a pathway to get back on their feet. So our mission was to serve and lift them from homelessness to independence, and these houses served as the foundation for bringing forth this change. The process was to put them in a transitional house, train them in a particular job skill and help them find full-time work with a livable wage and then, after six months move them to independent housing which we had built on abandoned lots in the city. We would then charge minimal rent until they got their feet on the ground, with the ultimate goal to sell them the homes within 3-5 years. So, in the course of a few years, they went from homelessness to gaining independence and self-reliance.

As a leader, you must think ahead and strategize ways to move the organization forward. Too many leaders are "firefighters" where they are constantly putting out fires by reacting to emergencies all around them. When these leaders figure out they need to stop managing the processes and instead allow their staff to work through the challenges with some advice and guidance, their organization or department begin to flourish. I call this being *proactive* versus *reactive*. Are you a visionary or a firefighter? Firefighting wears you down while being a visionary allows you to lead and bring excitement to all those who work at your organization.

At Catholic Charities, I was continually trying to think of ways to expand our services and reach more of the vulnerable population. I thought of a pregnant mother who needed a place to go and who didn't have adequate resources for a home to live in. I wanted to find as many wrap-around services as I could for these women. So I did a little research and found a home for expecting moms near our new office and decided to pay a visit to their executive director to see if she would be interested in partnering with us.

As I finished the tour of their beautiful home, we sat down and visited in more detail. During our conversation, she mentioned in passing that her mom had just moved in with her and her husband, but was having trouble finding a job. Curious, I asked her to tell me more. She said, "Well, I've never shared this publicly, but I'm starting to now. My mother has been in prison for 36 years for a murder she did not commit and recently, the governor of Missouri pardoned her and commuted her sentence—she'd been given 50 years to life without parole. We were so excited she was released, but she has very few options for living or working."

I was touched by her story and saw a budding opportunity. A few days later, I called the executive director back and asked, "We have a lot of people who come to us who are ex-offenders, and we find ways to help them build their lives back up and be self-reliant. My staff needs to hear about cases like your mother's. Would your mother be willing to come speak to our staff so we know how to serve this population better?" She wanted to talk to her mother and in the end, her mother readily agreed.

When her mom, Judy, came to our office and spoke, she left the whole staff in tears. Someone from our staff asked her, "Were you angry at your ex-boyfriend who framed you after he murdered someone and then walked away scot-free?"

Judy replied in a very succinct manner, "I was angry at first. But after a few years in prison, I decided that I could choose to be bitter or be better, and in the end, I chose to be better." The room fell silent. I was amazed at this woman's willingness to forgive and the joy she radiated to each person she encountered. She was a ray of light; and for me, as the CEO of Catholic Charities, I couldn't have asked for a better scenario to help establish the culture I was trying to cultivate.

Judy's words have stuck with me for a very, very long time. It's an iconic sentiment: *"I could choose to be bitter or better. I chose to be better."* Every time I think about it, I am moved beyond words. Judy, who had been unjustly convicted of a crime she did not commit, who survived prison and multiple attempts on her life while in prison, who managed to bring in the Bible ministry to the women prisoners and even embraced one of her would-be killers before she was released, was an exemplary woman who lived her Christian faith. She chose to be better in even the most unfair, difficult, and unbelievable circumstances.

Immediately after Judy's beautiful personal testimony, I asked her if there was anything we could do for her. She looked at me, laughed, and pulled out her smartphone. "Can you teach me how to use this thing?"

I chuckled and immediately realized that when she went into prison in 1982, cell phones and computers did not exist for the average consumer. She told me that while she was in prison for 36 years, she had not seen the stars in the sky nor Christmas lights. The things we had become accustomed to were foreign to a person who had been incarcerated for decades. I wanted to help and told her we could give her some training on computers and even her cell phone. As we were concluding our conversation, we prayed together and Judy shyly mentioned, "I could also use a job."

She was such a joyful person. She didn't have a drop of anger in her bones, despite everything she had been through. I talked to my staff about training for Judy and they were excited. I then decided to hire her at Catholic Charities as our part-time front desk receptionist to meet all those who came to our office. Judy was nervous as the telephone system was a little overwhelming, but she jumped in and learned quickly. Her bubbly personality spilled over to the staff and those who visited our office, especially the ex-offenders who had served their prison term and were dropped at our doorstep. People never had any idea she had been incarcerated all those years and were shocked to hear her story. Judy ended up becoming a great receptionist.

Her story is an incredible testament to how having faith in our God can help us weather the storms of life and give us strength, even in the most trying of times. I have walked the leadership tightrope many times where I tried to balance my work and family, but I realized, like Judy, that you have to keep your eyes focused on your feet while on the tightrope in order to make it through turbulent times. If you take your eyes away or give too much to your work, you lose your balance and you risk falling.

As a leader, you don't always get to spend time with the people who are extremely important to your organization and, within the nonprofit sector, your benefactors are your lifeblood. The opportunity to spend a few hours is rare, and I wanted to spend time with some of my best supporters. One of the best avenues I have found is organizing trips, and in the case of Catholic Charities, organizing a pilgrimage to Italy seemed like a great idea. As I was the host, I asked my local bishop if he would be our spiritual director. When he readily accepted, we began our planning a full year in advance and set up tours of Rome, Assisi, Florence, and Venice.

The pilgrimages I had hosted before—one in Poland and two in Austria—were amazing bonding experiences and I'm still in touch with some of the people we traveled with. So I wanted a similar experience with my community in Kansas City. But six months prior to our trip, in April, 2019, my wife was diagnosed with breast cancer once again. *Aggressive triple negative* breast cancer, which only 15 percent of people get. We wasted no time in lining her up for a mastectomy, lymph node surgery, and subsequent follow-up chemotherapy. It was just like how it had been earlier with her first cancer diagnosis. This time around, thankfully, there would be less chemo. But I was once again in the midst of doctor's appointments and chemo treatments while trying to run an organization.

During her cancer treatments in the summer of 2019, I received calls from three different people asking me to apply for the president's position at Ave Maria University. At first, I ignored them—my wife and our mission at Catholic Charities were my priority. I didn't have time for anything else. But after the third independent call, I thought, *Maybe the Lord is trying to tell me to be open to this opportunity. Maybe I should listen.* So after a lot of prayer and discernment, I submitted my resume in the middle of July. For the first time in my career, I didn't do any follow-up networking or reference calls like I usually did. I simply thought, *If the Lord wants this to happen, He'll make it happen.* I refocused all my energies back to supporting my wife and Catholic Charities where big things were beginning to happen.

My leadership strategy gave me the ability to run an organization and, at the same time, give my family all the attention they needed. I was not a manager; I never micromanaged people or told them what to do constantly. If you're a manager, things fall apart when you're not there. Because they've learned to rely on you too much to make all the calls and decisions, your employees may not have the confidence to move forward without your stamp of approval and everything comes to a standstill.

But at Catholic Charities, I was empowering my employees from the very beginning. I encouraged them to make decisions on their own so they would be ready to step up and lead when the time came. If someone didn't know what to do, I sat down with them and reviewed the situation together, figuring out where things went wrong or what mistakes to avoid. I'm proud that Catholic Charities had turned into a fruitful environment—and we had talented people who made the best use out of my leadership style. We had a great COO, an amazing CFO, a fantastic VP of Marketing, great fundraisers, and an incredible Chief HR Officer. These people made it possible for me to attend to my family during our medical situation. They stepped up when I needed them the most. Our mission and our vision united us—we were all working toward the same goal. So hiring the right people and coaching your team allows you, as the leader, to have the freedom to be a visionary. A great team can make all the difference. I saw it firsthand when my family and I were trying to cope with this serious medical situation.

During this time, we had already started planning for our pilgrimage as well. I had coordinated with a tour company that helped me navigate through the whole ordeal of planning the trip, putting together the brochures and the marketing material, figuring out the transportation, hotels, and everything else in between. In a way, throughout the cancer treatments, the anticipation of the trip kept my late wife motivated. She was worried the entire time that she wouldn't be well enough, that she would be drained with no energy and not have any hair. I reassured her that we really didn't have to do the trip—whatever she needed, people would understand. But as August, and then September, rolled around, things were starting to look up. She finished her chemo in early September and by the end of the month, she was ready to go and so was I.

My late wife on her last day of chemotherapy on September 6, 2019.

After months of planning, in October of 2019, 35 people from the local Catholic community, my wife, and Bishop James Johnston of the Diocese of Kansas City-St. Joseph in Missouri, started our pilgrimage. And it was an unforgettable experience. At every meal I sat with different people from our group and got to know them better; as a leader I made sure everything ran smoothly (I thoroughly enjoyed the task of orchestrating an enjoyable experience for everyone); and more than anything, the sense of camaraderie that we had cultivated as a community was one of the major highlights.

This pilgrimage stands out to me for one other reason: it was the last trip my late wife and I took together. And it was one that, in a way, came full circle; back in 2000, we had done a secular Mediterranean cruise from Rome to London on a beautiful 6-star cruise ship. That time, we had only a brief visit in Rome and couldn't really explore much, but she was so determined to see the Vatican that she managed to convince the bus driver to stop at a place where she could, at the very least, see it from afar. She had no idea how big it was! She had always wanted to go to Rome, but after battling another round of breast cancer with chemo treatments all summer, she never really thought it would be possible.

My wife's fears that she would have no energy were completely unfounded—she had more strength than I did! I distinctly remember this one day on our trip when I was amazed at her enthusiasm. We were in Assisi and after a long day (it felt like a long day even though it was only four o'clock) we got back to our room. I was exhausted—all I wanted to do was put my feet up and rest. We had walked 17,000 steps! Anyone would be tired after that.

I had barely settled down when my wife said, "I'm gonna go out and walk down the hill to San Damiano." I looked at her in shock; it was a mile and a half walk, not to mention, the climb back up the hill would be so much harder! There was no way I could handle that. But she went and managed to walk up and down the hill, which was another 7,000 steps, while the most I could do was stay in the room and rest. It was unbelievable that she had just come out of chemotherapy; her energy knew no bounds.

Assisi was the most beautiful place I've ever been. We ended up spending more time there because it was so peaceful and quiet, and the countryside had the kind of tranquility that you would never get to experience anywhere else. It was the complete opposite of Rome, which was a busy city full of people and noise. The quiet of Assisi gave us room to pray and reflect. If I could, I would go back there in a heartbeat.

Three days before we left for the pilgrimage, Ave Maria University wanted to conduct an in-person interview as I was one of their finalists. They wanted to fly me to Florida the day before we left on our pilgrimage for the interview with the search committee. But there was no way I could do that. I had a flight to Rome to catch! I thought, *I will tell them I can't make it, and if it takes me out of the running, I am okay with it.* Surprisingly, they rearranged everything and decided to fly me in two days earlier. I agreed and completed what I felt was an average interview. I didn't think the interview went all that well, at least not well enough to put me seriously in the running for the role. So when I got back home, I told my wife she had nothing to worry about— we weren't moving anytime soon and we could enjoy our pilgrimage.

We landed in Rome two days later, and it was beautiful. We toured the city on our first day and in the midst of all our excitement, I received a text from the Ave Maria University search committee—they wanted to talk to me further about the president's position at the university. I texted back stating that I wouldn't be available until Thursday; Most leaders face many distractions in their day-to-day work, but staying focused on the task at hand is so, so important, especially when those interruptions get demanding. I couldn't allow myself to be too distracted from the group I was hosting, so I literally put the university job out of my mind for the moment and focused on the people on our pilgrimage.

We toured the Vatican and all the major basilicas in Rome. We had an audience with the Pope where I was so close to him I could almost shake his hand! And there are simply no words to describe the beautiful works of art with Michelangelo, Bernini, and more. We toured the Sistine Chapel and numerous other beautiful locations in Rome while indulging in great Italian food and wine. From there we journeyed to Assisi to experience where St. Francis and St. Clare once walked and embraced the tranquility of that region. Not only was this an extremely fun experience, but it was so deeply spiritual. We prayed the rosary and attended Mass with our bishop every day and, at the same time, immersed ourselves in the food and culture of each region of Italy we visited. The experiences were incredible.

Our pilgrimage tour group in Assisi, Italy in October, 2019

It was in Assisi on October 10th that I received the expected call from Ave Maria University's search committee: they had voted to proceed with offering me the position as president and wanted to discuss what it would take for me to make the move. I was thrilled, but had to control my enthusiasm because of my personal situation with my family and my wife's recovery. The committee stated they wanted me to come to Florida to meet with the board of trustees and allow them to vote on whether to proceed. It was a wonderful, albeit unexpected, turn of events.

Here I am, on a pilgrimage in Assisi, and I am receiving a very clear message from God that I should take the job. My wife was recovering and her prognosis was good; all signs were in favor of me accepting their offer. I've always relied on my peace of mind and spirit when making major decisions. This was no different. I had spent time in each church I visited to pray and ask for God's will—not mine, but *His*. I finally made the decision to say yes, and then turned back to focus on the present: the pilgrimage.

As the host, I was responsible for my group. Even out of Kansas City, I was the leader, and that came with many duties. I had to make sure nothing got in the way of my group from having a beautiful spiritual experience. And by nothing, I mean *absolutely nothing;* I was very thorough about ensuring that the aesthetics of the trip promoted prayer, self-reflection, and solace, checking to make sure the food was good and met everyone's dietary needs, and herding everyone in the group wherever we went so that nobody got lost. You have to play a servant role as a leader. They all know who was leading, but when they see compassion, caring, and customer-centric focus in their leader, it gives them a sense of comfort. This was a humbling experience for me in a good way. I love to serve others and see Joy radiate from their faces. Servant leadership isn't easy; people come to you all time with problems, but no matter what problem they brought me, I immediately jumped to troubleshoot and find a solution. These were the sweetest, kindest people, and I enjoyed my role in helping them connect with their faith and God as much as possible.

Like many others in our group, my pilgrimage affirmed everything I was going through and my belief in my Catholic faith. We walked where St. Francis of Assisi walked, an incredible saint who publicly renounced all of his family's wealth and founded the Francisan religious order, which serves the poor while living a life of prayer, fasting, and penance. Many may recognize St. Francis for the phrase which has been attributed to him most often, "Preach the gospel at all times and, if necessary, use words." Seeing and praying in the Portiuncula, the small church St. Francis built 800 years ago that now sits inside the Basilica of St Mary of the Angels, was a powerful experience.

When we returned from our pilgrimage, my wife and I were both physically exhausted and spiritually energized, and I was feeling very optimistic about my new job at Ave Maria, especially since the timing of the call and pilgrimage were so intertwined. This new journey felt like it was ordained by God.

2019 had been a rough year for my family. As I reflect back, I was having great success at Catholic Charities as we were stabilizing with a new infusion of board members and key employees. We were growing, and I had our new strategic plan in place. I was elected by my peers to serve on the Catholic Charities USA Executive Committee and enjoyed all aspects of the organization. I had great employees, a great board, and great support from many people in the Kansas City area. In the midst of the turmoil, I was focused on the success of the organization.

Every single month of the year—except the month we went on the pilgrimage—was complicated by my late wife's health issues. She had fallen and cracked her ribs. She later had her second breast cancer diagnosis, followed by surgery and then chemo. So, by the time we returned from Italy, I felt we were off to a new chapter in our lives: cancer-free and a great new opportunity in Florida. I traveled to the Sunshine State in early November and accepted the job as President of Ave Maria University after a unanimous vote from their board.

My life was a whirlwind with wrapping up my CEO position at Catholic Charities while beginning to study details of the job as president. I had a lot of energy and excitement. On the Tuesday before Thanksgiving, as I was sitting in my living room in Kansas City reading emails, I received a phone call from my wife. Crying uncontrollably, she managed to tell me she had just been involved in a car accident. I jumped in the car with my son and went to the scene where she was still sitting in her SUV at a very busy intersection. I asked her what happened and she said hysterically that something was wrong, and that she never saw the car she hit in the middle of the intersection after she stopped at a stop sign. She complained of seeing floaters and colored lights in her vision. While thankfully nobody had been injured, something was definitely wrong.

So, on the Friday after Thanksgiving, I took her to her optometrist who performed a series of tests. When completed, he came out into the lobby and told me to take her to the emergency room immediately. The University of Kansas Medical Center completed a battery of tests and after 4-5 hours, the diagnosis came back: my wife had a golf-ball-sized tumor in her occipital lobe. They scheduled surgery for the following week.

The doctors said the tumor was likely unrelated to her breast cancer and that there should be no problem removing it. I was perplexed and wondered what God was trying to tell me and I was prepared to turn down the new job to focus on this new battle. My wife, however, was encouraging me to accept the job because she said everything was clear in our prayer. But at the same time, she kept saying, "I know that you're supposed to take the job and work at Ave Maria University as the president, but, for some reason, I can't see myself living there." She kept repeating that she was at peace and knew that this was the right decision. As I reflect back on this comment, it must've been a truly divine inspiration to her as we never would've guessed she was going to pass away two weeks after we moved the family to Florida.

But at that moment, the doctors told me all she needed was three radiation treatments and she would recover quickly. And so we kept moving forward. I continued the preparations for the move while I took her to all her doctor appointments and all of her radiation treatments. The doctors assured us that she was doing well and saw no reason why we couldn't proceed with my new job.

In January of 2020, after much reflection, prayer, and thought, I traveled to Florida to begin my new job. The family stayed behind in Kansas City so my son could finish his junior year in high school where he played baseball. Little did we expect 2020 to completely turn our lives upside down—an unprecedented global pandemic followed by a personal tragedy that would challenge me like I have never been challenged before.

New Town, New Job, New Virus, New Crisis

Higher education, nonprofits, and the corporate industry are three completely different worlds. Sometimes, people don't really see these differentiating factors because they focus on surface level elements. When I say I want to grow a university, corporate minds think in terms of profits and revenue, surplus or deficit, cost-cutting, and that's about it. Sure, these are important components, but they are just one of many that you need to be paying attention to.

I had to focus on many areas as the President of Ave Maria University—for our purposes here, I've narrowed it down to twelve, but there are likely more. The first and biggest one is, of course, the reason why the university exists: academics. Within academics, you work with faculty, tenure, research opportunities, curriculums, accreditations, and more. Tenure has been a very controversial topic in academia these days. Some people, typically in administration, oppose it because if you end up with a tenured professor who's "gone rogue," then, as an institution, you are very limited in what you can do. However, faculty are very supportive of tenure because it's a safety net that gives them academic freedom for teaching and research, and provides job security. By offering tenure, you keep really good, qualified professors for a long time; but on the other hand, it can also be risky for the institution if a professor's work declines over the years. In a corporate setting, unless you have a contractual employment agreement, all jobs are subject to termination at any time. If you're not a teacher, tenure isn't even something you think about at all!

When I was asked about this academic dilemma, I could see the benefits and drawbacks from both perspectives. I've always been a proponent of a hybrid system: an agreement where there's long-term job security for your great professors, but it still doesn't necessarily mean "forever." There are many creative solutions to level the playing field. But, as you can tell, it's a difficult position for a leader to be in. As a leader, making tough calls is a day-to-day task, so you need to develop critical ways of thinking, communicating, and implementing big decisions.

Academics is just one of the many areas presidents oversee. They deal with administration and staff, the financial side of education, IT, the Board of Trustees, fundraising, HR, marketing, enrollment, physical maintenance, and student life, including athletics—all very broad divisions with their own challenges, strategies, and skill sets, all separate budgets, and all extremely important.

Some small schools include athletics under the wing of student life, but I think it's an entirely different department. There's a lot involved in athletics that you can't see from the surface. To put things in perspective, here's the rundown: not only does the athletic director have to deal with numerous varsity sports and clubs, but he also needs to oversee the head coaches and the assistant coaches, plan and schedule the games, and manage all the athletes. As the president, I worked with my cabinet to approve plans or discuss strategies. So you can imagine how many meetings I had to attend, people, plans, and strategies I had to keep track of, and the sheer number of decisions I had to make. Upon my arrival, many issues had been put on hold as they were waiting for me to make a new decision.

In a corporate setting, you're not going to have as many departments to pay attention to. Instead, your focus is mainly on driving revenue, tracking finances, and selling products or services. You might have different branches of your products, however. For example, Apple has its iPhone division, MacBook division, iPad division, and other extras like AirPods and tech accessories. And within each of these, there's research and development, manufacturing, quality control, and more. As a CEO, you're probably looking at these overarching, interrelated aspects while also dealing with stock and shareholders.

So while there may be many departments, there's a sort of connection between them all, which is not necessarily the case with a higher education institution—for example, campus maintenance and HR are two completely different things, but you need to be nimble enough as a leader to divide your attention and yet stay focused. Juggling twelve different departments and managing all the faculty, staff, and students, while also reporting to the Board of Trustees was a tough challenge, but I had learned to master the balancing act. As a president, I had a lot of people reporting to me, and even more wanting answers.

Right from the beginning, I was working in tandem with the faculty, administration, and CFO, and empowering them to come up with solutions—they are given the responsibility because they are experts in what they do, and the mark of a good leader is to trust them to handle their departments by providing the support they need. For example, the provost at Ave Maria University was phenomenal at managing academia and faculty, and I relied on him to keep things running smoothly. Consequently, academics performed well because he consistently made the right calls, and I gave him the resources he needed to make it happen. That's why I'm a big advocate for having the right people in the right positions—as a leader, counting on your colleagues instead of micromanaging can really make a difference to the culture and lead to positive growth.

As a new president or leader of an organization, you're bound to inherit people. Sometimes, they're quick to adapt to the changes and harmonize with your leadership style. Unfortunately, there might also be people who may not understand or accept your vision and mission for the organization. Like we've talked about earlier, if you want your organization to succeed, you need employees who buy into your mission—not people battling you right up front, causing more delays and doing harm.

When I took over at Ave Maria, I had open positions on my cabinet. I had open positions for the Vice President of Advancement (fundraising) and no marketing department. Apart from that, there were other departments that were also struggling. But when you're a new leader, you want to be careful not to disregard what the previous presidents did. Until you're in their position for a few months, you don't see the whole picture. I was able to understand why the previous president was reluctant to fill these vacancies— he felt he shouldn't hire new people or go out to fundraise if he was not going to be in charge much longer. During the months before the transition, the entire university was in a state of limbo as the previous president was on his way out. So when I finally arrived and took over, everybody was excited to get started and put their projects and plans into motion.

As I evaluated the people I was working with, I saw how much time and energy they had devoted to the university. Some of them had been a part of Ave Maria for almost 15 years! Listening to their thoughts, concerns, and plans for the university, I realized that I was in the midst of some really great leaders. I looked at this nucleus of my incredible team and started to think about what I can build. But I wasn't the only one wondering what my next steps should be; *everybody* wanted to know what I wanted to do and how I was going to do it.

I highly recommend every leader not to give in immediately to this temptation, because you can get boxed in very quickly. Instead, take a step back, ask for more time, and evaluate the situation. You can share some things that can easily be accomplished, but be cautious of making commitments unless you have a full understanding prior. Give yourself a minimum of 90 days to listen, assess, and draw up an action plan. When people wanted me to come up with a full-fledged strategic plan and vision in the first few months, I refused. Instead, I laid out a 90-day plan of everything I'll be doing during that time. I wasn't interested in giving some kind of empty political speech about making ambitious changes that will never work out. I don't like making promises I can't keep. So I planned 90 days to formulate goals and step-by-step action plans. The first 90 days are crucial for you as a leader to understand what's going on and then come up with a mission and vision for your organization moving forward.

During those 90 days, I also met with a lot of people. I wanted to get to know everyone and hear their ideas. Those meetings gave me an insight into the culture of the institution and whether the departments were cohesive or divisive. In my situation, the board was very divided over the previous president. When I came in, I was voted in unanimously, but those who really liked the previous president's leadership were still cautiously optimistic and others planned to step down as soon as I was settled. By meeting with them, I got a broad understanding about the previous president's projects they wanted to keep alive and what changes they wanted to implement. You don't have to implement the things they desire if it is not what you believe will move the mission forward, but you do need to *listen*. So listening to the board and gathering information is crucial to your 90-day plan to help bring any board (or team) together, especially if they are divisive.

To keep in touch with the different departments, I initially held weekly meetings with my cabinet. Before every meeting, they would send me a written summary with updates from their division, allowing me to review and prepare for our meeting. In addition, I held one-on-one meetings with my cabinet members where we could discuss their areas of responsibility in more detail, initially every other week and then monthly or as needed. I would ask them, "What can I do for you?" to fully understand their challenges and priorities and see if I could get them the help they need.

Before I told them what we needed to do or laid down a deadline, which usually coincided with their priorities, I shifted my focus to team building. For example, we needed to hit a target of 500 new students enrolled in the fall of 2021 in order to meet our financial goals. Instead of "telling" my director of enrollment, "We need to get 500 new students this year," I asked them what their biggest issue was, and they would usually tell me they needed to hire two new admissions people to do the recruiting or other initiatives. So now that I knew what needed to be done, I was able to set a more sensible pace for us to move forward instead of just piling responsibilities on him. Those one-on-one meetings were great to establish that connection and open-door policy.

As you can imagine, trying to communicate with everyone in the university can turn into a *lot* of meetings. My advice for all leaders: *Be protective of your time.* You need time to gather and get your thoughts in order, which you can't do if you're in meetings all day. My protected times were in the mornings; I usually avoided meetings before 10 AM. At around 7:30 AM I would go to Mass, then get into my office and engage in thinking and writing time—vision time—and then at 10 I would begin my meetings. I've also found that my brain just shuts off after 3 PM, which means I need a break. Scheduling my breaks was very helpful and I recommend every leader to do so. Pay attention to your own productivity. This can help you leverage your extra productive hours in a day toward important tasks. When you're being pulled in so many directions, you have to be able to put up a firewall and block out some time in your calendar for yourself. It's all a balancing act.

Speaking of balancing acts, nothing tests your leadership skills more than when you have to make budget cuts. No one wants them and very few departments offer to cut their budget; so you have to make very calculated decisions. How you balance funding to continue current projects, raise money for new, and when to completely cut a project usually comes with contradictory opinions, oppositions, and sometimes support from your community.

Many colleges today are challenged with finances and enrollment. You know you have to make cuts, but it can be difficult. So many leaders today take the advice of corporate leaders who, not driven by the mission, fail to recognize loyal employees. They conclude that certain employees are not fit for their roles, so they might be the best ones to cut in order to save the organization. In a way, they are correct, but so often, this is never communicated outside the "budget cutting room." Many finance people focus on the numbers and try to figure the balancing act without realizing the overall impact. They look in the proverbial rearview mirror and make cuts accordingly, but this is not a great long-term strategy and frankly, many times, short-sighted.

I firmly believe there are two ways for a leader to get out of a challenging financial situation at any university: fundraising and enrollment. Both of these are growth-focused, positive to the bottom line and difficult at the same time. This is not the easy way out, and many leaders are not willing to risk setting goals that stretch beyond what they have already accomplished. When a leader or board makes deep cuts in the budgets, it rarely helps your university evolve unless there's a lot of waste. You certainly want to look for opportunities to curtail spending, but if the budget is lean, it's not always the answer.

Some leaders target cutting salaries and benefits, of which I am strongly opposed unless all other options have been exhausted. I believe in investing in your people and their commitment to your mission. In the end, you're not saving any funds if you cut employee benefits, you're just crippling your institution—those dedicated to carrying out the mission see the organization as not supporting them and the sacrifices they have made to keep the organization viable. There were numerous times over my corporate career where benefits were rising and I asked additional questions on how to resolve the issue. If you are presenting the same old material, it's probably going to increase, but if you get creative, you may be able to save money. I have done this numerous times and rarely did I have to tell employees we were increasing the cost of their benefits because I found ways to reduce waste with the benefits structure.

While I was handling all these new challenges, meeting with new people, and nearing the end of my first month, I started to read reports and hear discussions about a new virus emerging from Wuhan, China. I heard mixed opinions about it—some predicted it would spread to the US as well, while others were confident it would stay confined within the region it came from, like other viruses. As the days passed and we marched into February, I started to hear more about the COVID-19 virus and that it had entered the U.S. My students took their spring break during the last week of February, and that's when things began to escalate. COVID was spreading rapidly in the United States and as president, I was faced with making hard decisions in an unprecedented situation. A global pandemic was upon us.

CHAPTER
SIX

The World Doesn't Stand Still

Before the pandemic engulfed us in a very difficult situation, I'd made good progress in getting accustomed to my role as president. I had approved the launch of a new marching band program sponsored by a generous donor. As a kid who grew up watching great marching bands at Lawrence High School and the University of Kansas, I felt no university with a football program should be without one or at least without a pep band. Ave Maria University never had a marching band before, so I saw this program as a way to create new spirit and energy on campus and provide an opportunity for musically-talented students to get involved and explore a new avenue.

When you step into a new leadership position, you don't just have the opportunity to make changes and start new projects—you also need to fix the things that aren't working. A serious issue I inherited was a fieldhouse that had critical structural and environmental issues. It was recommended that it could no longer be used in any capacity—that meant no orientation, commencement, basketball, or volleyball games. It eliminated football and other sports' locker rooms and no all-school gatherings could be held in this space. It was a huge blow to the university since it had used the fieldhouse as a large part of all its campus activities.

I was initially assured that we could make it through commencement, but then we would need to shut it down and begin repairs immediately. I needed to prepare for a major fundraising campaign for the fieldhouse and initial estimates were coming in at over twice the original cost to build just 10 years prior. I was still searching for a vice president of advancement to lead our fundraising efforts, particularly for this new initiative. Not having a vice president of advancement in place for over a year had brought most fundraising to a halt, with only one experienced fundraiser who had secured gifts of over $10,000. In addition, the university only had one full-time marketing personnel, and they had very little experience. So without hesitation, I hired a new vice president of marketing from Catholic Charities of Kansas City-Joseph. I knew he understood my vision and would relate to the mission of the university.

This issue with the fieldhouse was hardly the only thing on my mind at that time. As a new president, I needed to meet with board members and prepare for fundraising events and meet many of our great benefactors. I had to prepare for my inauguration at the end of March. I inherited an executive assistant from my predecessor who had committed to stay with me until I could find a new assistant, but after my first week, she decided to submit her resignation. A day later, she walked into my office and asked if she could rescind her resignation, to which I agreed since I had no issues with her and no one to step into the role. She expressed a desire to retire *before* my first board meeting in February and in the short term, her uncertainty filled me with apprehension and some anxiety as I was trying to settle in.

On the personal side, I had to get my family (who were still in Kansas City) moved, and since the doctors kept assuring me that my wife was healing very well, I felt comfortable waiting until after my son finished his spring high school baseball season. We had to figure out the timing of the move along with selling the house, finding a new home for the family in Ave Maria, scheduling a moving van, and more. My wife complained of dull headaches and blurred vision, but doctors assured us that this was normal after a surgery of that kind. All these responsibilities were converging when I first heard about the pandemic, and my internal support system at the university felt weak at best.

There was a truckload of information slamming into me at full force—it was hard to even grasp the magnanimity of it all. I'm sure this was a shared experience among all leaders. For university presidents especially, the stakes were higher as we were dealing with a diverse population of students, faculty, and staff, as well as the students' parents.

During the last week of February, when my students left for spring break, the COVID-19 pandemic was beginning to dominate the news and staff members were asking for advice. I started convening our staff to discuss the next steps. We hadn't had any positive COVID cases in the student body or on our campus, so I made the decision to keep the campus open and bring everyone back after spring break. The following Monday, classes went on as usual, and we continued monitoring the situation daily. I established a new coronavirus response team (CRT) to report to me each day.

In the first full week of March, things took a turn for the worse everywhere—mass panic spread across the country as cases started to rise. But at the university, we were still at zero positive cases on campus and in the town. I continued to read and study the facts and figures on the Florida Department of Health website, the CDC website, and more, where I could drill down my data to every county and town to determine the number of positive cases. There were very few overall cases in the state and even fewer in our area. Everyone was doing okay physically, but I could sense the anxiety was starting to affect everyone. Every day, people asked me what my plans were and every time, I would tell them, "We are open but will take precautions." I continued to plan for my inauguration at the end of the month.

When other universities decided not to allow students to return to campus after their spring breaks, the pressure began to mount. I distinctly remember hearing from my son that the Big 12 conference basketball tournament and the NCAA basketball tournament were canceled. That's when it truly hit me that this was *real* and a bigger deal than anything that had happened in my lifetime. Our Ave Maria University men's basketball team was vying for a return to the NAIA national tournament when we received notice that their season was being canceled as well. I continued to convene my cabinet, and, of course, they looked to me to provide answers on how to move forward each day. One major question was whether we should shut the campus down and allow students to return home, or if we should continue to hold classes until a certain number of positive cases hit our campus.

My thoughts were this: the students were back, and we were a small community. Since our spring break happened so much earlier than others, whatever they might have gotten and brought back had already happened. Students were coming into close contact with each other every single day—living in the residence halls together, the large student-athlete population practiced and worked out face-to-face on a daily basis, sat in class together, and ate in the cafeteria. And yet, we still had no positive cases. What benefit would sending them home do? Unless the data called for it, I could not see any reason why we needed to close down at that point.

I began to meet daily with my internal coronavirus response team to help me make these decisions quickly. I was debriefed on important data coming in from the CDC and the Florida Health Department, I looked at the stats in our local area, and made calls based on the information I had available. I started reaching out to other presidents as well to discuss their plans and see what they were doing. I did everything I could to get the best understanding of the situation as it unfolded to keep our school safe.

I also had to share responsibility for our students studying abroad in Rome where positive cases were rising. I was in regular correspondence with the study abroad program directors and their college president in Rome, and we were trying to find a way to get our students back home. We waited as long as we could as we observed Italy and, more specifically, Rome, being shut down to the point we had to get our students out. I followed every student's travel progress for a return until I knew they were safely back on U.S. soil. I was also praying constantly and talked to my family back in KC as they were very nervous about all the news they were hearing. My wife's immunity was compromised, and we feared she would be at risk. Nobody had ever experienced a situation like this before. It was chaos, high stress, and constant concern. A crisis was upon us, and no one knew what the next day would bring.

When you're a leader, you don't always know whether a decision, especially a time-sensitive one, is right or wrong. One incorrect decision could cost you everything. Our university hung in the balance for a number of reasons. One day, as I was fielding calls and emails from parents, faculty, staff, students, and the local community, I was able to have a brief conversation with a mentor of mine at another university in the Midwest. I asked him how he was making decisions, and I remember his advice: "You know, Chris, sometimes you just have to make a decision. You can't wait. Right or wrong, you've got to go ahead and make a call. Make a decision *now*. Don't worry about tomorrow."

He was right. You can't hesitate. And if your decision is wrong, you can try to change it tomorrow and hope it wasn't to the detriment of those you are responsible for. Each day and each night I would pray for guidance, then study the data, talk to my cabinet and other teams, and then make an informed decision. The next decision I made was to cancel the inauguration and rescind 1,500 invitations. We needed to allow people to cancel flights, hotels, and other travel plans. We had a full day of festivities planned but quickly canceled all of them, including all our food vendors. I was disappointed, but it really wasn't a tough decision at this point in the pandemic. I didn't want to take the chance of having a super-spreader event due to my inauguration.

Our students were going to class for a second week, and we still had zero cases. I had my staff check with the local health clinic to see if any positive cases had shown up there. Zero. Some students asked to return home, and we agreed to accommodate them and study remotely. They left their belongings in their residence halls because we were hoping this would be a short-lived virus. By the end of the second week, it was becoming obvious that the fear had escalated to a level that was not mentally healthy nor sustainable to keep the students on campus. I convened my cabinet on a Friday morning and asked my provost how quickly we could convert to online classes if needed. We did not have any type of robust offering for online classes other than in our graduate programs and even those were minimal. This was a big risk.

Although these days it's hard to imagine a world without Zoom, Microsoft Teams, or virtual meetings, in 2020, they were mostly unprecedented. My provost assured me that if I made the decision to move to online classes, we could be ready to go on Monday morning. I was blown away by the preparedness of our team! I knew it couldn't have been easy.

Meeting virtually provided the alternative to in-person classes we needed, but I still wanted to honor those students who wanted to attend in-person classes. Could we do a hybrid model? Parents called in with concerns that the virus was going to explode on our campus and their kids would be trapped; others contacted me telling me to be strong and keep the campus open; and some students were scared that if they stayed, they could potentially infect someone when they returned home. There were so many contradictory opinions to filter through.

Popular opinion was trending about 70-30 to keep the campus open, but I was concerned about students contracting the disease with harmful effects. And, of course, the potential financial disaster for the university when students no longer on campus want a refund for tuition (along with room and board) that could put the whole university at risk. It wasn't just about the livelihood of our school and staff—the local community's restaurants and shops depended on the student population for their businesses. If they all went home, it could spell disaster for them too.

In other words, people's lives and jobs were at stake, and I felt responsible for all of them. I gathered students in the chapel to pray and assured them that we would get through this together. I could see fear in many of their eyes and some were crying. As a leader, I had to assure them that I was acting in their best interest and things were going to be okay. I talked to them about the fear of the unknown, how we had to place our trust in God, and reassured them with the infamous Roosevelt quote, "The only thing we have to fear is fear itself." In the meantime, my family was at home, and my wife continued to complain about headaches, dizziness, and blurred vision, but the doctors kept assuring us that these symptoms were normal. We set up a virtual doctor's visit with her surgeon at the end of March.

In the midst of all this, I needed strength to stay upright: I was praying all the time. Most of all, I prayed for wisdom and guidance. In our staff meetings, I made informed decisions after a lot of analysis, but they were only "today" decisions. I told people that things could change quickly, as statistics and data had been morphing every day. With so much new and changing information coming in, I knew we couldn't make fixed, blanket decisions. It had to be day-to-day.

But we did take one bold step forward. After meeting with my cabinet on Friday morning to discuss going online, I made the decision: keep the campus open for students who wanted to stay and go to classes and offer a remote option for those who wanted to go home and complete their classes online. The hybrid educational platform fit everyone's needs. My provost quickly organized a Friday afternoon meeting with the faculty where I met with them to give them my decision to have hybrid classes. When I finished my talk about how we were going to navigate all of this, they gave me a standing ovation. I was relieved. I was very impressed by how the faculty were incredibly prepared for it too. They were not just prepared but also equipped and organized—I pulled the trigger, and our hybrid model was put into action immediately.

At this point, I made the decision to fly home to be with my family. My son's high school baseball season had been postponed, so we were waiting to see if he would play again. We were all in limbo, and I felt I could work from my home in Missouri. I remember boarding my Southwest non-stop flight from Ft. Myers to Kansas City with only five passengers on the whole plane. I laughed because we had five crew members who told us to "spread out" in normal Southwest humor. Ten people on a Boeing 737 was a memorable experience—it was like I had my own private jet!

Back at the university, the first week of the hybrid classes went well. We still didn't have any cases on campus, but as cases escalated everywhere else, we had to change course once again as students were beginning to leave Ave Maria en masse. There were too many students going home and not enough staying on campus to make it work, so we decided to scrap the hybrid model until the situation got better and moved to a completely virtual setup. My advice to leaders everywhere: *be nimble*. Situations can change rapidly, so you need to be able to dodge, turn, and keep moving forward. That's exactly what I did at Ave Maria University. While all classes were held online, students were still living on campus—they lived in their dorms, ate in the cafeteria, and even attended daily Mass that we still held every day outside.

We never forced our students to isolate themselves within four walls. I recognized that human interaction was crucial, and we could figure out how to stay six feet apart. In a time of such uncertainty, pressure, and change, not having a sense of community could've been very damaging to their mental and emotional health. As humans, we're made for each other, for discussion, for touch, for community. Seeing

20 people on a computer screen could never really fulfill those needs. As a leader, you need to be very aware of the human aspect of every decision you make. It always has an impact on your clients, employees, and students, on their personal lives and productivity. I was very intent on keeping as many social events as possible and tried to bring a semblance of normalcy to the university environment by ensuring students and faculty could connect over food in the cafeteria or spiritually during daily Mass.

When everything transitioned to online-only with students still on campus, and we realized the situation would probably not change soon, I talked to my spouse, and we decided it was finally time for my family to make the move to Florida, especially since my son's baseball season was officially canceled. We made the appointment with my wife's surgeon to discuss her condition to make sure all was okay, and through a virtual conference, he assured us that she should continue to get better and it was okay to move. We visited with her oncologist, who said she would help find new doctors and a cancer clinic in SW Florida. So we found a realtor and a moving van company, packed up, and moved the family to our new home within two weeks. We rolled out of Kansas City on Good Friday, and since all the churches were closed and no services were being held in the Kansas City area, we set our sights on landing in Ave Maria on Easter Sunday morning. With my family and pets in tow for the 21-hour drive, we decided we could make it in two days. We drove late into the night and arrived in Ave Maria on Easter Sunday morning at 1 AM, caught a few hours of sleep, and ventured out onto the campus to attend Mass.

My wife didn't feel great, but we figured the long trip had just exhausted her. She went back to the president's condo where we were staying until our belongings were delivered to our new home, and she rested the whole day. The next day, she didn't feel any better and stayed in bed. I called my personal physician in Naples, who asked me to bring her in so he could evaluate her. He gave her a prescription and told her to continue to rest.

Unfortunately, two days later, she was progressively worse. So my physician recommended I take her to the emergency room in Naples (about a 30-45 minute drive), which was an experience in and of itself because of COVID. I had to drop her off and then they would not allow me to join her in the emergency room. I was asked to wait in the car. I called my physician, and he began calling his contacts and trying to sort it out. 15 minutes later, I was asked to enter through a side door so I could be with my wife in the ER, who was scared and alone. All the regulations and hoops I had to jump through just to be in the room with her were exhausting, and I was thankful I had a great doctor to help me as I knew she needed my support and advocacy. Shortly after I arrived in the room, she lapsed into a very confused state. When I asked her my name, she replied with a string of numbers. She didn't know where she was or why she was there.

Every time I asked her for the names of her kids or her mother, she would recite numbers. I began to pray the rosary, and as I prayed the Hail Mary out loud, she began to recite it perfectly, right along with me. I stopped in amazement and asked her my name again, thinking she was back to normal. She couldn't remember and gave me a string of numbers again. I began to pray the Our Father, and she recited it perfectly too. I repeated this over and over while we waited for the ER doctor. Even through what was undoubtedly a very strenuous situation for her, her faith was still shining strong. What we sometimes feel may be boring "repetitive" prayers, had now become something she could rely on. It was all she could do. I recorded my interaction with her so I could show the doctors. The doctors ran some tests, but no one could figure it out. I sat beside her, praying. They admitted her to the hospital for further evaluation and I, once again with the help of my great doctor and approval from the CEO, worked my way into the hospital to stay beside her.

But leadership never stops—not even when you're in a hospital room. I kept getting calls, texts, and emails from the university asking me to make a decision, approve a plan, or navigate a situation. So I sat there with my laptop and a phone, trying to troubleshoot and coordinate. We had a board meeting coming up and I needed to stay on top of the COVID situation and monitor our numbers. My executive assistant was refusing to come into the office until after hours and was working remotely. She was fearful of getting the virus and taking it home to her family, so she kept threatening to quit because of the stress. There were so many complications that needed my attention—it was escalating. If there was ever a time to learn that empowering your team to make decisions is critical, it was now. They were still used to the previous president's leadership style and didn't want to make any decisions without my approval.

At the same time, I realized I wasn't just a necessity to the university, I was also a necessity for my wife and family. I was her conduit for communication. It was a difficult situation where my role as a leader in my personal life was at odds with my professional life. My family was calling, friends were texting, and I was just trying to juggle it all. I learned the technique of copying and pasting texts to make things quick and simple. My oldest daughters took the responsibility of keeping other family and friends informed. The family needed me and the university needed me—all at the same time.

With the agreement that I would not leave the room, I slept the first night at the hospital with her. We had one nurse on the floor in charge of a large number of patients when my wife began to deteriorate even further. I called the nurses' station numerous times with no response. I finally opened the door to the room, stood by the entrance to make sure I didn't violate my agreement to stay in the room and asked if I could get some help. The nurse finally came and began to chastise me for not staying in my room, and then she chastised my wife, who was not coherent, for pulling IVs out of her arms and not eating her meals. Obviously, the nurse was not handling her stress well, but she had no support. I was upset but kept calm.

By that evening, my wife seemed to be resting well, and the hospital told me I had to leave at 7:30 PM. I headed home to be with the family, who were living among boxes; we hadn't even had time to unpack yet. My older children had arrived to help with the younger ones, so I had comfort knowing they were being taken care of. I got a few hours of restless sleep. The next morning, as I was eating a quick breakfast and preparing to head back to the hospital, I heard one of my younger daughters talking to my wife on the phone. We were blown away! She had snapped out of her incoherent state! It was a miracle!

I rushed back to the hospital, which took about 45 minutes, and when I got to the room to begin the discharge procedure, I was admonished by the head nurse for being in the room. I learned that during the night, this nurse strapped my wife's arms to the bed so that when she woke up, all she could do was yell for help. I explained to the nurse that my wife had yelled for a solid hour before someone came to help and this kind of care only reinforced my need to be in the room. She didn't care and reported me to the head administrator, who came into the room with threats. Learning from my leadership roles, I was calm and explained to her that I wanted to visit with the CEO; I just wanted to take my wife home, and I would never return to this hospital again. She finally relented and discharged my wife.

Once we arrived home, she sat down at the dining room table of our new home and enjoyed a bit of dinner but had no energy and asked if she could retire back to the condo. The next day, she wasn't feeling well again, so I called my doctor. He was concerned and said if she wasn't better he would admit her to a different hospital. Our chaplain for the university came by the condo to see her, heard her confession, and then gave her holy communion and the anointing of the sick. She tried to eat a little lunch but was too weak.

I took her to the new hospital in Naples for more tests, but when she started to lapse into incoherent states of mind again, the doctors moved her to ICU and decided to do a spinal tap. I continued to try to work from the hospital room when my assistant called to say she was resigning. I sat there in disbelief. Couldn't she understand and see what I was going through? Why couldn't she wait until the board meeting or commencement was over? More challenges arose as I had just made the decision to hold a virtual commencement and my board was insistent to meet in person in two weeks regardless of any circumstances. The pressure was mounting, but it was still not the worst.

I will never forget when the doctors came into the ICU room and shared with me that they had discovered a high level of protein in my wife's spinal fluid and said it was likely brain cancer. They recommended chemotherapy immediately and stated that if we agreed, she could perhaps live another six months, but if not, she had about three weeks. Weeks and weeks of agony came down to this. Against every desire in her body to not go through chemo for a third time, she chose to proceed with putting a stint in her head so the doctors could administer chemo. It was painful, but all she wanted to do was to see her family again.

I went home and informed the family of the dire situation and did my best to be optimistic. When I announced the diagnosis, my oldest son immediately realized her condition was terminal. For the sake of the younger siblings, we didn't go into detail. The next day, they took my wife to surgery to put a port in her head and gave her the first round of chemo. She was consciousness for a while, and I was hopeful, but she kept complaining of severe headaches, so I tried to assure her the chemo would take a little while to have an effect. I fed her a little breakfast, and I noticed she was starting to fade off mentally. The hospital staff came in and quickly moved her back to the ICU. Shortly after, I requested a priest to come to give her absolution, and since she was not coherent, he gave her an apostolic pardon as well. The next day, they moved her back to her room and as the 3 PM hour on April 30th arrived, I started to pray the Divine Mercy chaplet when my doctor came in and joined me. He checked her vitals and then gave me the hard news that she was not likely going to make it another

24 hours. I was shocked. The only good news I received was that my assistant stated she had returned and would work until after commencement.

I called the kids and put them on the phone with her to say their goodbyes. I called my chaplain at the university to come to the hospital. At 4:41 PM, I was praying the rosary and holding my wife's hand when she took her last breath. At the exact same time, my wife's phone received a text from our 14-year-old daughter. She'd sent a picture she had worked on for three hours of Jesus holding a child with the words at the bottom, "Well Done Good and Faithful Servent" (sic). I was in total shock from my wife's death but amazed by God's grace of comfort through my daughter's exact timing with the picture. I knew at that moment that the veil is thin between heaven and earth.

The drawing my daughter texted to my late wife at the exact moment of her passing.

I had no time to grieve. I had to plan a funeral (which was complicated because all churches were closed), look after my children, prepare for an upcoming board meeting, deal with all the challenges COVID brought with it, and had to compose a speech for the commencement. But through it all, I felt a spirit of calm. I firmly believe it was the Holy Spirit that was giving me the strength to keep a clear mind during a major tragedy. It was a testament to the prayers my family and I received from everyone around the globe. My faith kept me grounded and gave me hope. If there was ever a time to fall off the tightrope, it would have been now.

When you're a leader, you can't control a lot of the storms around you, and it was especially difficult when that storm was the pandemic. In the education field, COVID took a big toll on teachers and professors—55 percent of educators wanted to leave their jobs sooner than planned because of the pandemic.[2] When you're in leadership, mental exhaustion can be severe. Even Dwight Eisenhower struggled as the president of Columbia University, according to Michael MacDowell, the president of Misericordia University in PA, "Even though he had led thousands of troops in the greatest war of modern times, overseeing allies from different countries and cultures, while managing the likes of Patton and De Gaulle, whose egos sometimes outstripped their usefulness, he still found university leadership defied even his most capable management skills." As a five-star general, Eisenhower was certainly familiar with bureaucracies, yet he found the idiosyncrasies of selecting internal university leadership perplexing. He recorded in his diary, "There is no more complicated business in the world than that of picking a new dean within the university."[3] And he never experienced a global pandemic of this magnitude!

No wonder the turnover rates for university presidents are so high. They have gone from an average tenure of 8.5 years in 2006 to, according to some statistics, a 54 percent rate of turnover for presidents in the next 5 years.[4]

For me, as a new president in a new community and town, the stressors were mounting. But the respect, support, and compassion of the people around me and my faculty and staff at the university gave me strength. Not to mention the Lord; I was praying on my knees a lot to ask God for the strength and wisdom to persevere. I never despaired; I always had hope. I always felt strongly that things would get better. That faith became my guidewire and helped me stay balanced on the leadership tightrope. Because of my faith, I never felt like I was going to fail or fall.

While the university gave me a bereavement leave, there were still important decisions that needed to be made, the biggest one being the commencement. Since the fieldhouse was still unavailable, we decided to do it virtually and planned to pre-record the ceremony to broadcast on that day.

We held my wife's funeral on May 4th, which was performed by the university chaplain inside an empty church with my kids, my brother and his wife, and a good friend's family. My pastor was insisting on a limit of only ten people inside the 800-seat church. I asked him which one of my kids should we leave outside because I had 11 (me, my seven children, two spouses, and one granddaughter). He didn't respond, and I told everyone, including my brother, his wife, and my wife's great friend's family, to just walk in with the casket and not stop. Everybody had the right to be there. We all deserved the opportunity to grieve properly and no pandemic was going to stop me from allowing my family to do this.

Sometimes leadership takes courage, and this was one of those moments. I tried not to be angry because my wife deserved a large funeral and felt they could at least allow 16 people inside the large and spacious church. It was a beautiful funeral that my children planned with music being played off my son-in-law's iPhone. The next day, May 5th, I came into the office to prepare my commencement speech and some last-minute preparation work for the board meeting—which was scheduled on the same day as my wife's burial with no plans to reschedule, even with my request to do so. "The university has important decisions to make and we can't delay," I was told. So I sat down to start typing up a draft of my commencement speech. I was still reeling from my wife's funeral the day before, trying to plan how to get the family to Nebraska for the burial and trying to focus on the work at hand when I got a call at around 10 AM. It was my provost, asking me if I was ready to give the speech. I told him I was getting there, but in reality, I had barely given it much thought. He said, "Good. See you in an hour," and hung up.

In an hour? I had gotten the dates mixed up! I didn't even have the speech written, let alone rehearsed. I dove in and typed out a speech in 30 minutes. I donned my new presidential robe for the first time, put the presidential medallion around my neck, and walked over to the auditorium for filming. I was on autopilot. I went up on stage and delivered a speech that came straight from the heart. People told me it was powerful and inspiring. And I lend it all to prayer. The title of my speech was "We Can't Stop Living."

Picture taken right before I gave my first commencement speech as president at Ave Maria University.

I don't really remember much of it, but I felt like I had been trained for this. All my experiences and previous roles had prepared me to take charge, lead, and succeed, even when I wasn't 100 percent mentally all there. I didn't think; I just moved and tried to keep from breaking down into tears. It was like my baseball days when I visualized myself in the eye of the storm, the center of calmness, a grounding image that helped me sail through and move forward. I was focused in a way that came with leadership experience. I was in the zone. Later in the week, I moved forward with an interview with Fox News host and EWTN anchor, Raymond Arroyo, to continue to share updates and give publicity for the university.

As for my commencement speech, I realized that even though I was in the midst of my own tragedy, I needed to rise up and inspire others with the hope that we can keep moving on.

We can't let a virus stop us from living our lives.

We can't let a death or a tragedy stop us from moving forward.

The world keeps spinning—and we have to keep moving forward as well. God is with us. We will not despair; we will prevail. This was the essence of my speech.

Finding
Strength
in My Faith

Early in the week after the burial of my wife in Nebraska, I received a call from my board asking if I planned to make an announcement about the Fall 2020 semester and if we were going to be open. I was barely into my bereavement leave, but the university couldn't wait. I told them that we were going to be open for in-person classes and I would have my provost send out a letter stating this. I was not going to mandate that students *had* to be vaccinated to return in the fall. I believed in the freedom to choose for numerous reasons and since we had zero cases through commencement, I knew we would be okay.

I also knew we had to prepare, so I turned it over to my cabinet to begin implementing safety procedures throughout the campus, including provisions for quarantine if needed. We were going to play a full season of fall sports and try to return to normalcy. The good news was Governor Ron DeSantis had passed legislation allowing us to make these independent decisions. Other universities, like Notre Dame, were requiring all students to be vaccinated. I wanted to give my students, faculty, and staff the freedom to choose (we would later be rewarded handsomely with the second highest enrollment in the history of the university, which was followed one year later with the highest enrollment in history).

I also had to begin the process of finding a contractor to repair or replace the fieldhouse at the university. I started working remotely and when possible, meeting people on campus. We were going to be open and we had to get back to fundraising, especially since there were so many financial unknowns in the near future. That summer was quiet as the town was deserted and the campus was empty. Many times I felt alone and had a lot of time to reflect on my grief, but in this situation, I masked the grief by pouring into my work.

I focused on the task in the midst of the storm, and was devoted to opening our doors for the Fall 2020 semester.

I knew we would not be able to stay at zero cases forever, especially since all of the athletes were required to be tested frequently. Our staff prepared expeditiously for this and I was confident we were going to make it through this wave of the pandemic. We set targets and measurements and if the cases escalated to a certain number, we would evaluate all the details of our protocols and see if we needed to go back to online classes. When our first positive cases were reported in August, one of the doctors we had called to examine our COVID-positive students in quarantine made an observation: physically, students were all doing okay with almost no symptoms, but their mental health was suffering. Many of these kids were experiencing anxiety and depression due to the lack of socialization and he said the isolation was doing more harm than the actual disease itself.

As we moved throughout the fall, we were doing quite well. We did all the proper procedures with distancing, cleaning, masks in the classroom and meetings, and the energy from the student body was positive. I had hired a new assistant and the rest of my cabinet were doing well with me officially back at the helm. We were completely back to normal and cautiously optimistic that the worst was behind us. We still took precautions and made accommodations for students and staff who needed them, but overall, the craziness of the pandemic had begun to die down. I was nonetheless prepared for an uptick in cases; I told my cabinet that it wasn't a matter of "if," but a matter of "when" it would happen. The peak hit in October with about 75 positive cases and we were prepared.

The decisions I had to make during this time were far from being easy. 2020 tested my strength and put me through trials and tribulations that I could only overcome with the Lord's guidance—my faith helped me stay on that leadership tightrope. I took everything to prayer before I made major decisions as grief was zapping my quick recall and short-term memory. I prayed and prayed. My morning and evening prayers were for wisdom, strength and right knowledge, and for the resilience to get through the tough times. Whenever there was a monumental task, I trusted God to lead the way and help me make those right decisions because I knew if it all depended on me, I was in big trouble.

As a leader, you inevitably receive a lot of criticism for your decisions and in the middle of a crisis, the "arm-chair quarterbacks" come out of the woodwork and critique everything you do. But you have to ignore the noise and lead. You can't worry about the chatter, you have to focus on results and leading your organization to bigger heights. If you get caught up in the noise, you will forget your mission. You can't react, you must *lead*. Your organization depends on it.

On campus, we had a beautiful Eucharistic Adoration chapel. Whenever I needed quiet time to pray and reflect, I would go there. I would wake up at 3 AM on Fridays and take my golf cart up to the chapel to just sit in silence and reflect. There were days when I couldn't even function enough to pray—but that was okay. God is present at all times. He never leaves. Those moments in that chapel with Him helped me gather the strength and wisdom to persevere.

I would also take early morning and late night walks across the campus where I would pray the rosary or do some quiet reflection. I read books and listened to uplifting music on my earbuds. I never stopped going to Mass, not even for a day. Those were just some things that balanced out all the stressors in my work environment. Every leader needs to take that time to recalibrate and reflect. Whatever your faith may be, these daily check-ins are imperative for staying connected and grounded to it. If you're a morning person, wake up a little sooner so you have a few moments of peace and quiet before you go about your day. Or take advantage of your evenings and turn off all your electronics and TV to read a book or write something. Do what works best for you, but always have some time for yourself full of prayer, reflection, and quiet. Giving myself to prayer has always helped me make my best decisions.

This isn't unique to the year of COVID. Even as a little kid and especially during my college baseball career, I have never forgotten the Creator who made me and gave me the talent, because He could take it away at any moment. Praying everyday, thanking God and asking for guidance and strength has helped me move forward, even during times when I couldn't *see* the way forward. We don't always know what's out there or what our future holds. For me, praying has always been about trusting and nurturing that hope that things will get better and I will find strength to persevere.

And God did grant me strength, especially to help me navigate my personal life. When my children lost their beloved mother, I had to put my own grief aside and look after them. I mourned the loss of my wife, but they were also suffering greatly. As their father, it was my responsibility to do what I could to support them through such a difficult time.

I still had two daughters and two sons at home, and I found that being a single father while also working as the president of a university during an unprecedented global pandemic was not an easy task. I gained a whole new respect for single parents raising young children. My work and my children needed my time, and it wasn't always an easy balance. But I kept praying, and the Lord guided me and reassured me that everything was going to be okay. My faith gave me the hope to endure. If Christ hadn't had hope that there was something better on the other side, He never would have suffered like He did on the cross. He knew and set an example for us. And that's what I have: it's hope. Hope that something better is coming. Hope is the light in the darkness. Hope is the light at the end of the tunnel.

People often talk about ROI, return on investment, in work settings and how it's crucial for good business, but as a leader, you also need to have ROL—a return on life. Taking a vacation, spending a meal together, or just watching a movie with your family—if you don't make these adjustments and take a break from the challenges of day-to-day life, your ROL will begin to fail.

At this point, it was beginning to fail for me. I could see my children struggling to cope with their loss, but I didn't have the time to help them through it. During COVID, it was very hard to find counselors who would travel 30-45 minutes to Ave Maria. The girls did not want to do virtual meetings, so it took some time to figure out. I didn't have time to get counseling for myself, either. Even before COVID, it was hard to find someone who specialized in grief—it was impossible to find a grief counselor who could meet face-to-face in our small town.

Of course, we weren't alone. I met with a priest for spiritual advice when I had the time, and we also had many people supporting us through our grief. I was touched by our community who provided my family with meals or took care of my girls. The one thing I had to learn was not to say "no" to help. Leaders are often bad at asking for and accepting help—but it's not about *you*. Allow people the grace to be able to help you. Whether it's pride or stubbornness, you need to relinquish it and accept help because it can help you shift your mindset.

So as the Spring 2021 semester started, I had high hopes and great anticipation as things at the university were looking up with the highest spring enrollment in history, and time was beginning to heal wounds. My two sons moved back to the midwest, one to live with my older daughter and the other to finish his senior year in high school. We were beginning to manage the virus on campus efficiently. We were setting new records for fundraising in a fiscal year and we had record applications, record deposits, record acceptances, and we would eventually have the largest enrollment in the history of the university in the Fall of 2021.

We had our commencement in May of 2021, and I felt energized and renewed as any leader would with all the great things happening. I, with the help of my cabinet, were able to present to the board the first balanced budget in years and were on target for having a surplus for one of the first times in the history of the university. As we rolled into summer and as I was preparing for a few days of vacation with the kids, I received a call from my board chair who shared that the executive committee had decided to pursue a merger with another institute of higher learning—

and I quickly realized that I was not in a personal position to move the university through a merger.

Mergers are usually very difficult to navigate as you try to merge cultures, and they create a world of uncertainty for employees wondering if they will keep their jobs. I had been through mergers before and knew I couldn't dedicate enough time and energy to work 18-hour days to make it happen. Even if I was able to, I couldn't do that to my daughters. Now, more than ever, they needed me. So on the 12th of July, I turned in my resignation and stepped down as the president. I had always stated that family is before work, and this time I meant it. So, the board and I came to a very amicable agreement, and I resigned to focus on my family while agreeing to serve as a special consultant in the interim to the new president. After my resignation, I was able to spend much more time with my two daughters. I had to find a new place to live and began to search in earnest. As a single dad, I was tasked with responsibilities I'd never had before.

Especially since my girls were teenagers, we were all treading new waters together. I had to do the work of both a mom *and* a dad and have conversations with them that had usually been "mom's territory." Not to mention navigating the emotions of two teenage girls—well, let's just say dads aren't usually very gifted at that. But as I spent more time with them, I learned, and we developed a much stronger bond. I had great friends who gave me invaluable advice. I tried my hardest to bridge the gap between us, and focused on affirming their femininity rather than forcing my own interests on them.

In August, for the first time ever, I took my daughters to a hair salon right before school started. I didn't realize you could spend $250 at a hair salon! But after I paid the bill and as we were walking out, I saw my daughters' happy smiles, renewed self-confidence, and lots of selfies, and I thought to myself, *This is the best $250 I have ever spent.*

My two youngest daughters.

I was blessed to have the opportunity to share these moments with them, and I'm thankful for God's guidance in helping me prioritize my family. Leaving Ave Maria was one of the toughest decisions I've had to make, but once I did, I knew it was the right call. I drew a lot of wisdom from reflecting on the life of St. Joseph, the earthly father of Jesus. He was a man who, through many trials and hardships, never wavered in his commitment to God and his family. He was also a businessman and trained Jesus to work with his hands and guide him through life. Some people hang posters on their walls of Michael Jordan, Tom Brady, or some other star that they admire, but I keep a statue of St. Joseph in my office at all times to remind me of his servant leadership. I find it funny that people often depict St. Joseph as an old man—but as Mother Angelica, who founded the largest Catholic television network in the world, EWTN, once said, "Old men don't walk hundreds of miles to Egypt through a desert!" His model of fatherhood, humility, and servant leadership has always been close to my heart, and I try to live by his philosophy of leadership as much as I can.

Empathetic or servant leadership to me is transformational. It's not easy for people, especially leaders, to sit quietly and listen. But as a true servant leader, it's your job to listen, be humble, have empathy and jump in and do what's necessary to help others succeed. Like St. Joseph and St. Pope John Paul, St. Mother Teresa of Calcutta embodied the spirit of a servant leader. They showed us how to be successful. Mother Teresa took care of the poor and showed others how to do it. She demonstrated and led—that's what servant leadership is about. A lot of people think servant leadership is weak and that people will walk all over you, but that's not true at all. Meek is not weak. You can be a great leader by being small—Mother Teresa was meek, but she spoke in front of dignitaries and stood up (at only five-foot-zero!) for the truth. She won the Nobel Peace Prize and immediately after said, *Okay, let me get back to work.*

Some leaders think they need to control everything and everybody and put fear into people to get them to perform, but that's not true leadership—that's called management.

Leading by example is what gets you results. You need to be humble and you need to employ transformational practices if you want to make a difference. Derive strength from your faith and lead by example, both in your professional and personal life. The results will speak for itself.

CHAPTER
EIGHT

Building Something Bigger Than Myself

During baseball practice, I would always take time for visualization before I stepped into the batting cage or on the field. This was a part of my routine. As a left-hander, I would spend time visualizing the perfect swing, hitting a line drive over the second baseman, or imagine myself hitting a homerun with an easy swing. Where there's competition, there's pressure: you're in a position where you need to perform, and in baseball and other team sports, the entire team depends on you. Athletics can be great preparation for high-pressure situations both in your career or personal life. When tragedy strikes, you need to be prepared. You can't predict when, but you know it will eventually happen, especially if you are in a leadership position.

College baseball prepared me for many instances in my life. Many baseball players practice hitting and fielding with a lot of repetition, while actors in theater practice their lines and stage movements over and over, but few people take the time to visualize a positive outcome. During the heat of the competition, you may feel the intensity of the crowd, but you have to focus without being distracted. Instead of focusing on the noise, the chatter, or getting distracted by the mounting tension, you need to prepare in advance to calm your nerves. I prayed throughout games, in the on-deck circle, in the field, and at the plate. I would also use the visualizations I practiced each day when needed; it cleared my head, preparing me for any tense moment I would encounter.

Sometimes, my prayers and visualizations are more about centering myself—to take my mind to a place as far from my current state as possible. You can create the most relaxing place you can imagine and then reflect on it. My visual has me sitting on the ground leaning against a tree, overlooking a lake with a snow-capped mountain range in the background, a slight breeze and crisp mountain air flowing through my nostrils. I would breathe in and breathe out slowly. and I would be perfectly calm. This visual, in the past and even today, always calms me down and gives me the tranquility to think and reason in difficult moments.

I believe this is what has led me to set the career batting average record for NAIA. As I write this book, that record is still intact, even after 37 years. I've used that visualization process ever since college and it has calmed me in the midst of all the noise and chaos, and helped me make the right decisions, lead other people, and gain control of my life in a myriad of circumstances. I still use it religiously to help me succeed in my career and personal life. Even when times were cloudy and I could not see a clear path ahead because there was so much going on in the outside world, retreating into my visualized place of calmness helped me reorient, gather my thoughts, and march ahead.

The year after the onset of COVID-19, In 2021, I needed calm more than ever. I needed time for prayer and reflection. After I resigned from Ave Maria University, I finally had the time to reflect on the past two years of chaos and process the tragedy of losing my wife after a 5-year battle with cancer. I had so many successes in the midst of all this and I could do nothing but sit back and marvel at how great God was at providing a clear path so frequently. He opened doors I could have never imagined and through the chaos, I heard the calm voice of reason, but there was still the exhaustion of giving it all to my job and my family. So when I stepped down as president, I needed to decompress from everything that had happened. I moved with my family to Orlando with the hope that change would bring good things.

But I'm not one to sit idle—I actually enjoy working to see things succeed. A couple of my friends gave me suggestions that opened up a series of doors for me: they said I should start coaching and consulting executives to give advice based on my experience as a leader. Two friends in particular had coached executives for years and they were both very successful, and they gave me a lot of great tips on how to make this happen.

They explained to me that now more than ever, great leadership is necessary and CEOs and presidents don't know who to turn to during these challenging times. COVID disrupted every single industry—and what executives *thought* they knew about their industry. Now, when the paradigms have shifted, they needed a sounding board who could also give them valuable advice.

When you're in a high position in a company, it's hard to know who you can trust. After all, how can you expect your direct reports to always give you the best opinions and advice? Going to your board members for advice can sometimes be challenging because they begin to question your ability to lead, when in reality, you are being honest and vulnerable. We know we don't always have the answers. Many executives battle with the vulnerability that comes with asking for help. They fear it might make them look weak, when in actuality it just shows that they value diverse opinions and perspectives. But sometimes, employees, and especially some board members, expect leaders to know *all* the answers—so who can they turn to now?

With my multi-faceted experiences in different fields, from insurance to higher education to non-profit to entrepreneurship, I have collected strategies, wisdom, and experiences that could be valuable for any leader looking to grow and nurture their company or organization. One of my good friends, Lamar Hunt Jr., has told me many times that my best virtues are my authenticity, approachability, and relatability. My single-minded focus on getting the job done while also having a sense of humor, he thought, would help me be successful in a coaching role. And I realized that throughout my life, working at all these different industries, my favorite parts of the job have always been the training and coaching component. I knew that by starting Ice Executive Coaching and Consulting, I could make a difference and build something bigger than myself.

Getting my company started was a lot easier than I had anticipated and I had a lot of encouragement from one of my own coaches. She gave me the confidence to take a risk and push forward, and was extremely patient with me. All my experiences linked together to help me find a successful launch strategy. I loved the flexibility—after spending a year in higher education where you had to jump through hoops for every decision, having my own company came with a pair of wings that freed me and gave me much-needed agility. But the biggest gift this flexibility gave me was the opportunity to take the time I needed to get my two daughters settled into our new home.

When I launched Ice Executive Coaching, I was focused on helping for the sake of helping. A lot of leaders need someone who would listen to them, and I was ready to fill that void. My vision for my company started to materialize: I want to help CEOs and executives navigate the changing, challenging times and develop their leadership styles to fit their organization, and even change the culture of their organization if needed.

I'm a big advocate for transformational leadership. My technique of changing the culture of an organization is to focus on the mission and strategize the changes that need to be made to turn that mission into a reality. In my experience, most leaders who face challenges or struggles are not looking at the root cause closely enough: their failing company culture.

The culture is unhealthy when it's not aligned with the vision; the culture is only culture when *everyone* is on board. It's not something you include in your business plan and call it a day. It can be difficult to navigate, but it's a task leaders must take on if they don't want their organization to crumble. Too many organizations bring in a manager to focus on the financial situation alone, swoop in, and make cuts at the detriment of the employees. Obviously, the financial situation is critical to success, and as I have stated before, "No money, no mission." Making major cuts is typically a big corporate model to satisfy stockholders for short-term returns, but it doesn't work well for many organizations where budgets are already tight and employees' salaries are not excessive. Leaders need to step in and look at the long-term solutions.

In some companies, employees are constantly looking over their shoulder, they're afraid of their jobs, and they're scared to speak up. These are tell-tale signs of a toxic culture. It usually stems from managers and CEOs thinking they can threaten people to get the job done, and while it might work in the short-term, it causes lasting damage to the company. No wonder those organizations see a lot of turnover and low employee retention rates. I would also say that many of these managers don't handle stress well and take it out on their employees instead. As you notice, I call them "managers," not leaders.

People mistakenly think that managers and leaders are the same. This couldn't be further from the truth; managers and leaders are fundamentally different in their leadership styles. Leaders create a vision while managers create goals. Managers try to control situations to reach their goal and see people as working *for them*. They don't have the solutions; they copy the competencies and behaviors of others and never adopt their own leadership style. Instead, if something is not working, they simply eliminate it—in the case of employees, they fire them. Managers focus on systems and processes while leaders focus on relationships.

Leaders have a vision and people follow them. A leader tries to figure out exactly what's going wrong, and if there's anything they can do to help employees find a solution, whether it's by listening to them or providing the resources they need. Leaders coach, managers give orders.

This is not to say I've never had to let people go; when I first became a leader, I realized that sometimes, when your employees are not aligned with the organizational mission, the only option left is to remove them. However, I encourage all leaders to first determine whether their employees are capable and willing to change. If they are, then it's only a matter of leading them in the right direction. Sometimes, all your employees need are resources and a little bit of coaching to be successful. It's on your plate to check in with them, figure out what they need, and provide it so they can be successful.

When I started at Ave Maria University, the marketing department consisted of one person with very little experience and a budget of only $30,000. At a university that generates $50-60 million in revenue with 1200 students, there are typically 10-12 people in the department and a much larger marketing budget. So, I hired the person who had worked with me during the rebranding efforts at Catholic Charities in Kansas City. Kevin Murphy is stellar at marketing and I trusted him to do the same phenomenal work at Ave Maria University—he was a guy that could work magic, even with a minimal budget. He asked for a few resources and performed beyond my expectations.

But even a genius can't do much with so little money! He trusted me to help him find additional funds, and even when the pandemic hit and we had to make budget cuts, we found some additional money and a generous donor to help as well. Once he had some resources, he was able to put his superior level of work into action and really managed to transform the university with new messaging and marketing.

When I advise leaders, I always tell them that hiring the right people is like choosing a relay team. Everyone has their own strengths and their own positions. Once you hand over the baton, you've transferred control, and you have to trust them to bring the organization closer to success. And when you win, it's because you've all endured and succeeded together—it's not about you, it's about teamwork. A coach never runs the race, only shows them the vision of what it's like when you win with a huge celebration at the finish line.

When I was working in insurance, one of my managers told me, "Hire people who are better than you." He said they would help me cover my weaknesses, and I could cover theirs: a patchwork of strengths and weaknesses that could help us succeed together and raise our organization and me to new heights. At my previous jobs, I always asked my direct reports what they wanted, and what *I* could do to help them reach out and get it. You need to hire great people and instead of suppressing them just because they're "better" than you, you need to allow them the freedom to run and succeed. Give them all the tools they need, train them, and help them improve and grow daily. It's all about nurturing them to develop into their roles. I found out when I did this, promotions for me and my people came at a high level.

Great leaders rarely need to micromanage people. You hire them because you deem them capable and talented, so let them take charge of their work, especially at the executive level (entry-level employees need a lot of training and coaching early on, so they might need more initial scrutiny). This will also free you up to focus on big picture agendas, lead teams, and create a better working environment for the whole organization. You need to be the visionary, not the manager.

Most of my clients who come to me have one overarching problem in common: it's almost always people. A lot of organizations see high turnover rates, but they have no idea why. Typically, their organization's culture is to blame. Maybe the wrong people are in the wrong seats, employees aren't able to fully exercise their strengths, or the culture is just toxic and limiting. Sometimes, employees just don't feel connected with the leadership and vision. As their coach, I walk leaders through some questions:

- Where is the problem originating from?
- What's the misalignment?
- What resources do you have in your arsenal that can help you mitigate this?
- How do you help your people align with the vision?

Usually, everybody thinks it's all about the finances. Most of the time though, it's really only a smaller element in a bigger problem. You can cut all the programs you want, but if you don't have people, you can't operate. And if you're cutting resources, they can't be effective. So it's a matter of fundraising to get money for the betterment of your non-profit organization and your employees or finding new sources of revenue for your for-profit corporation. It's important to ask questions and find answers. While it might all seem cut-and-dried, any leader who's been in a tough spot knows that sometimes, you need someone to guide you—to be a pillar of support. For my clients, that's where I come in as the executive coach.

Leadership is not a "one size fits all" situation. Different organizations need different types of leaders at the helm. Your leadership style has a big effect on your company's culture, productivity, and growth. But that doesn't mean there's a "wrong" or "right" type of leadership—each style comes with its own pluses and minuses. One thing I have always noticed in my career, and especially in my executive coaching organization, is that the culture reflects the leader.

Your leadership style isn't inherent. You develop it over years and years of your career. That's why you don't typically put a new entry-level employee in a leadership position as soon as they are hired. They neither have the experience nor the self-awareness to properly lead your team. As you accumulate years of experience working in the industry, you become more acquainted with your own leadership style. You understand what works and what doesn't, and through trial and error, you find strategies that help you lead your teams. I firmly believe that you must also read books, attend seminars and conferences, and hire brutally honest coaches to help you determine your leadership style, because sometimes we are blinded by our own egos. By the time you're in an executive leadership role, you may have a good idea of your style, but again, it doesn't come naturally and like any great professional athlete, you must continue to learn and grow. That's why companies that grow organically and promote from within have excellent leaders in place—they are nurtured carefully, and they understand the culture and grow into their career.

Leadership styles come in different shapes and forms. You might be a humble servant leader, a passionate leader, an extrovert leader, an introvert leader, an outward facing leader—they are all equally valid and conducive to your organization's growth. But the key is to identify and understand *your* style. It might be surprising, but most leaders have no idea what their leadership style is. One of the first things I do with my clients when I sit down with them is to ask about their style. If they don't know, then I help them figure it out. Having this awareness of how you function can help you be a better leader.

I've always identified myself as a transformational leader. I'm not always sure why God calls me to certain leadership roles—at Federated Insurance, my own hospice company, Fransiscan University, Catholic Charities of Kansas City-St. Joseph, Ave Maria University—but these opportunities made it very clear to me that helping people and organizations grow is what I'm meant to do. I am a transformational leader in the servant leadership style. I help people find their strengths, and I'm really good at reading people and working with them. I try to get the right people on the right seats on the bus when I start, so we can go on a successful journey. As an executive coach now, I aim to help other leaders do the same at their own organizations.

When I meet with leaders, CEOs, and executives at Ice Executive Coaching and Consulting, my mission is to help them be more effective, influential, and successful. I train them to lift not only themselves, but also their people. By empowering your people and your clients, your success is unlimited. Through my company, I equip leaders to be successful, and help their teams to grow stronger. When people worry about competition I let everyone know that

I firmly believe that "a high tide raises all ships." When people are successful, others follow. The positive energy that flows from the top is conducive to success at all levels. Organizations need great leaders to be bold and courageous, not trying to conform to everyone's desires. I am grateful for the opportunity to help organizations thrive and reach the pinnacle of prosperity, security, and stability through my coaching and consulting abilities.

A LEADER IS MORE THAN JUST A JOB TITLE

The most valuable, insightful, and affirming feedback I had ever received came from a visit to Ave Maria University in late 2022. My resignation was old news by this point, and during the course of my trip, many people approached me, commending my leadership during the chaos of 2020 and 2021, and the changes and decisions I made at the university when I was president.

One person from the community that rarely had any type of conversation with me during my tenure, and was not affiliated with the university, said something that stood out for me: "Of all the leaders I've seen come and go at Ave Maria University, your leadership made the biggest impact because, unlike others, you were visible in public all the time, approachable, and community-oriented. You were *with* the people, your staff, and the students, not staying locked up in your office during some of the toughest times for our community."

His appreciation left me speechless. I was struck by the magnitude of difference I had made by being an empathetic and very public leader. I realized students, faculty, and people in the community felt heard and seen because I gave them the opportunity to talk while I eagerly listened. It struck me then, more clearly than ever, that being a leader is more than just making big changes or implementing complicated strategies and churning a profit—it was about really, truly leading by *listening*. I recall always being amused by a few people in the community who stated they never saw me in public. My research always concluded that they were the ones who were staying at home isolated—no wonder I never saw those critics. Funny how that always seems to be the case.

Leadership is not an easy task. In fact, even if it seems easy on paper, it almost never is. When you're being pulled in multiple directions by demands and deadlines, it's hard to be available. But that's exactly why it makes such an impact when you are. As a leader, you need to orchestrate time and space to meet with people, connect, and listen. That's why my 90-day plan at the university and Catholic Charities started with a lot of listening sessions; without those, I would've never been able to identify the divisions within the boards, the mistrust of the faculty and staff, and the students' fear that their voices weren't heard.

I was exhausted at times, but still found the energy to go to a community member's home and share a few spirits and a cigar, even though I rarely smoke. I had faculty members come to my home to share their thoughts and we would sit by my pool and discuss the issues of work and life in general. I would invite groups of students to my home so we could connect and I could hear issues that may not come up in a formal gathering. I would have conversations with all of them, get to know them on a personal level, and listen. If you don't listen, you won't even be aware of the problems within your company or organization. If you fail to catch those issues before they pile up, you can be sure everything goes downhill from there. Listening is key if you want your organization to remain steady and strong.

Now, let's go beyond your organization's bottom line—listening is about enriching yourself and the people around you. There are great leaders all around you, and you're only one deep conversation away from gaining invaluable advice. But we often fail to make the move and ask. I've always asked leaders in my network or organization if I could take them out for coffee or buy them lunch. Over a shared meal or beverage, I would receive their wisdom and insights. It was a simple matter of asking questions and listening. All leaders want to share their success stories, talk about their experiences, and help you get a deeper understanding of what it means to really succeed. You just have to be willing to listen.

I remember meeting with the president and CEO of Federated Insurance when I was a young, new marketing manager. I was invited to his presidential suite after hours one evening, along with his senior vice presidents. I went there unassuming, but in awe that I was in the same room with many of the top leaders of my company. I didn't talk much; I just listened, fascinated by the collective knowledge and experience that filled the room. There were great conversations all around me about how we could take the company forward, new ideas that could improve efficiency, novel ways of doing things.

I stood silent, listened, and absorbed all this information. I gained a lot of new perspectives that day, but my most important one hit me when somebody asked me what I thought. At that point, I was only a mid-level manager! I was still new and didn't have much experience. But the leaders there wanted to know my perspective because I was the one on the front lines with our marketing team and interacting with the clients every day. "You're important," they said, "and we want to know how we can help you and give you the resources you need to excel."

As I talked and shared my ideas, they simply listened. It was empowering to me as an employee, and I could tell they found my perspective just as helpful. It was a mutual respect, a mutual give and take. As I grew into my leadership position, this incident was constantly at the back of my mind. I ingrained that philosophy into my own leadership style. I've always made time for my employees to communicate. You need to allow that time as a leader—how else do you stay connected to all the different aspects of your company? Staying confined to your office and giving out orders is not what makes you a leader—it's getting involved, listening, and empowering your team that makes a difference in the organization.

By connecting with employees, and especially the leaders in your organization, you not only gain information and diverse perspectives, but you also build a network of people who hold respect for you and want to see you succeed. Gaining that kind of trust and support is priceless. But the only way to be a genuine leader is through empathetic listening.

You learn a lot when the walls come down. Whether you're a leader at your company or at home, if you listen well enough, you get a deeper understanding and build relationships in ways you never thought possible. My conversations with my 17 and 14-year-old daughters opened new perspectives for me in my personal life that I never knew existed. One look at the relationship I have with my older daughters compared to my younger ones reveals the marked difference true listening makes.

My late wife was more involved with the older children than I was—she was the one who talked and listened to them the most. Now, as a single parent of my younger children, I'm involved in every facet of their life. We have talks about school, friends, boys, sports, and music, and as I listen, my daughters' walls come down and we bond on a level I did not even think was possible before 2020. We had open, honest conversations about their grief, regrets, and how they felt when they lost their mother. It occurred to me that these conversations would've never happened if I hadn't taken the time to sit down and listen. I might've never developed the bond I have with my daughters today if I hadn't made time for them in my schedule. It wasn't easy with everything going on at the same time, but the effort was well worth it.

The Ice Family in 2021.

In my career as a leader in various industries, I've come to appreciate the gift that is listening. Every piece of advice I've compiled in this book is a result of this. I've gained ideas, information, and wisdom from listening to those who are successful in their own leadership journeys. I sat down with my managers and listened to their experiences, I had private meetings with my staff, with the local community leaders, and ate lunch with students in the cafeteria to listen to their take on the university and what changes they would like to see. Today, I sit down with my clients, listen to the problems and issues they're facing in the workplace, and work with them to find solutions. Listening is the mark of transformational leadership.

As a leader, you'll always face tumultuous times and tragedies—that's part of the job description. If you haven't experienced a crisis or chaos, be prepared: you will. You've read my story, you've seen the tragedies I've had to overcome, and you've gained insights into how I managed to navigate them successfully. As a leader, when these challenges come, you will make a decision on whether you will take the challenge head on and grow, or ignore it and ultimately fail.

In race car driving, when there is an accident in front of you, they teach drivers to drive right at the accident and not to try to avoid it. If you try to avoid it, you will get caught up in the carnage on either side. If you drive right at the origin of the accident, by the time you get there due to the high speeds, the accident will be dissipated on the track and you will avoid any major catastrophe. The same goes for leadership. You must address problems as they arise, listen to the issues and make decisions. The longer you wait, the worse it may become.

If nothing else, I hope this book helps you become a better leader in your work, your personal life, and help you master the balancing act between family and career. I always encourage my clients to not be afraid to walk that leadership tightrope when times become challenging, as they often do. People depend on you to go out on a limb without showing any fear. Staying focused on the task at hand, having the right philosophy, mindset, and faith can help you stay steady and not fall off the tightrope. Being a leader is difficult work, which is why only few aspire to be a leader and fewer yet actually take on the task. Sharing my story will help you see that this can be most rewarding when done right. Remember, leaders are not born, they are made.

Now, begin your journey. Work hard, listen, and go make yourself a great leader!

ACKNOWLEDGMENTS

This book never would have happened without the encouragement of many people. I am especially appreciative of Mary Gardner who helped me believe I could write this book, gave me great advice and provided support all throughout this process. She was not just a cheerleader, but a great coach and friend who nudged me forward to the point of completion. I also appreciate the support I received from my children and their spouses, Katie (Ryan), Kassie (Nick), Nathan, Jacob, Michael, Therese, and Julia, who have all walked this journey in life with me. Their patience and prayers for me over the years, and especially while writing this book, have allowed me to fulfill another dream: being an author. I am blessed beyond measure.

NOTES

1. Josh Howarth, "Worldwide Daily Social Media Usage," Exploding Topics, January 9, 2023, https://explodingtopics.com/blog/social-media-usage.

2. Tim Walker, "Survey: Alarming Number of Educators May Soon Leave the Profession," National Education Association, February 1, 2022, https://www.nea.org/advocating-for-change/new-from-nea/survey-alarming-number-educators-may-soon-leave-profession.

3. Michael McDowell, "Your View: Why even military hero Eisenhower struggled as a college president," The Morning Call, January 25, 2022, https://www.mcall.com/opinion/mc-opi-college-presidents-turnover-macdowell-20220125-dcmwolubungirobcgrpx4xzxiq-story.html.

4. Justin Zackal, "Riding the Wave of College Presidential Turnover," Higher Ed Jobs, April 5, 2022, https://www.higheredjobs.com/articles/articleDisplay.cfm?ID=3013.